Grateful Heart 2

MEMOIR

OF A

CANCER SURVIVOR

&

ACTIVITY JOURNAL

*Wishing you a life of blessings,
love + abundance — Shannon Knight*

SHANNON KNIGHT

Grateful Heart: Memoir of a Cancer Survivor and Activity Journal

Copyright © Shannon Knight 2018

ISBN: 978-1-7320321-2-5

www.shannonknight.com

CMN Hospital (Alternative Cancer Treatment)
www.cmnact.com

♥ *Dedication* ♥

To my son, Kyle, and my daughter, Jessica. I am most grateful for your laughter, which tells me you are happy and everything is alright in your world. My truest days of gratitude are the days you were born. My appreciation for you only grows over time.

- Love, Mom

♥ Acknowledgments ♥

First and foremost, I would like to thank God for the many blessings I see more clearly now in my life. During the process of putting this book together, I realized how writing has been a blessing for me because it opened a door for me to show my appreciation to others and to be grateful for the smaller things I took for granted. I am aware more than ever that none of us are promised today so we cannot take people for granted and we need to show them love.

To my lovely mother, Alicia: I thank God for you. Thank you for your strong, soft shoulder. I can come to you even today for comfort. I am sorry it has taken me so many decades to clearly see what a blessing I have had with you as a mother. You stayed at home with five children while dad was working and going to school. Wow, is all I can say. Thank you for being the best mother and spreading your love around each day to all of us kids. It's a daily commitment, one job you cannot abandon even if you are sick. You taught me any grace and elegance that I have; you taught me everything there is to be a lady—even though that seems to be going out of style, I hang on to that. I have strength, too, which I got from you; you never jumped ship with all of us kids! I wish as children and especially as teenagers that we were capable of understanding what that was like for you. The years would have been easier for you if we understood what a challenge being at home with five children was while your husband was gone 80 percent of the time to get the bills paid and food on our table. You are the greatest, and I am blessed to have a mother as loving as you. I hope this book warms your heart, Mother.

To my inspirational father, Robert: I thank God for you. Thank you for your positive mindset with all of us. You always saw the glass half full, and when I think of optimism, I see you as a great example of showing us that we could get through the hard times. You were not around a lot because you had to support our family and you missed so much while all of us kids were growing up. When you were around, wow! You taught me art, somersaults, and what plagiarism meant at a very young age when I lacked confidence in my own writing and decided to copy verbatim all the information about honey bees off of the back of a honey can for a book report! Who knew this lesson would be so valuable at this stage in my life and one of the first lessons I taught my own children. I look forward to sharing all of the good that comes from this book with you! Thanks for not just believing but knowing that I could do this!

To my daughter, Jessica, and son, Kyle: You are the best things that I have ever done in my life! You welcomed me into motherhood, and I am so grateful for the lessons you taught me. When I first looked into your eyes, I had hopes and dreams of being the best mother to you both. I started learning at age 21 what it felt like to have two people I would give my life for. You gave me something to work for. A good life for you is all I want. It's funny, this feeling I have of my heart being outside my body with both of you and now with the precious addition of your own loves, their families, and the blessing of grandchildren.

To my two brothers and two sisters: I am forever grateful for all the wonderful memories growing up together. We loved, we fought, and goofed around a lot together. Those are the blessings in my heart I carry around with me! All of you are part of who I am today. You helped shape me into a woman I like being. Sometimes I will say something funny or inspirational and hear one of you in my mind. Each of you has inspired me in many ways. Our fights only showed me later on how close we were to get that annoyed with one another! It has never lessened my love and gratitude for you in my life! We were a big family living in a small apartment or small house and received many benefits of learning teamwork, love, forgiveness, and tolerance. How can I forget all our together times playing in the backyard, making up plays and dances, finding stray cats, playing kick the can, getting grounded, and even getting sick together. Poor mom had her hands full with us kids passing the flu, chicken pox, mumps, and measles to one another. We also passed love and compassion though. I remember stories of defending each other. We were all in it together, even though there were the times of separation. We were creative as kids who did not have a lot of material things growing up, but we figured out ways to have fun in the neighborhood. I wouldn't change a thing and am so grateful for each of you.

To every single person who has been touched by cancer: It is astounding how many people have reached out to me because they refused to give up when all seemed hopeless. Your courage and tenacity inspired me and reminded me of my own cancer journey. Many people contacted me on behalf of a loved one. I thank you for your graciousness during those calls. You were vulnerable and open with me on such a sensitive matter. I never knew if I was going to say something that may unintentionally hurt your feelings. It is a chance we take when we engage in a conversation with someone who is scared and in need of support. I never want to hurt someone and am grateful for you silently forgiving me if I misspoke or handled any moment of our conversation awkwardly. I pray during and immediately after our calls. Thank you for sharing your stories with me. You laid them on my heart, and they stay with me and teach me gratitude. It's important that you know how tenderly you touched my life and helped me develop more compassion and empathy. I am forever grateful.

To Dr. Edgar Payan and the entire medical team at CMN Hospital who took care of me when I was being treated for stage 4 breast cancer. When the doctors in the United States made me feel that surviving it was hopeless, you restored my faith. You encouraged me continually. You saved my life with a far healthier approach than conventional treatments. I learned that miracles still happen, and you showed me that it could be done without chemotherapy. When you saved my life, I tried to thank you, and I will never forget your humble response when you said, "No, no, no, Shannon, do not thank me; thank God." I continue to do just that with each day I wake up. What a blessing to be alive. You are a bright light—compassionate, gentle, and caring. I am grateful for the existence of such a doctor who spends time with all of his patients. I admire your sensitivity to each person and their feelings, your humbleness and persistence to keep trying with every patient.

To all my other family and friends, who I could not possibly mention each by name: Thank you for your love and support through fundraising, letters, gifts, and for lifting up my spirits during the most challenging years of fighting for my life. I am alive today because of your love. Even when some of you distanced yourself because you were afraid or just felt awkward. I know how hard it was for you to be around me sometimes, and I know each of you coped with the stress of it all in different ways. I am grateful now because I have learned over time that you were going through something, too, while I was sick. Some of you showed love by pushing your ideas on how I should try to win my battle over cancer. Even that was love. You each showed it differently. Thank you for cheering me on and helping me feel comfort, even with the little things like getting me a Slurpee to help me with nausea, helping me with bathing, blow drying my hair, and even the stitches on my chest to stop the crazy itching! Thank you for playing cards with me, watching movies with me, writing me letters, and just being there by taking a phone call. Thank you for believing in miracles. It is all the little things that made me feel loved. These are the moments that I will hold dear in my heart forever. All of you deserve halos and capes for being my heroes and angels. All of you were such an integral part of saving my life and giving my life new meaning and purpose.

♥ Table of Contents ♥

♥ *Preface* ♥

I always knew the day would come when I would write a book to share my story with others who are going through cancer. I battled breast cancer twice and was naive in thinking I needed a happy ending before I shared it with people. I missed the point altogether of how important it is that we share with others what we are learning along the way. I learned that "Happily Ever Afters" could be obtained daily. I started realizing this when I began practicing gratitude. Once my attitude changed about my circumstances, I began to see more miracles take place in my life. *Grateful Heart* will take you on part of my own unpredictable cancer journey and show you how I transformed over the years from a very frightened woman who felt hopeless to a woman who felt new meaning in her life.

Cancer has changed my life profoundly. I had to make some necessary attitude adjustments so I could learn to view the trials and adversity in my life with a new perspective. Cancer was not the only hardship I faced, and I know there are others who will have gone through additional obstacles, as well, which makes it even more difficult to find gratitude. I had to find a way to heal my heart first. I had to put a plan in place to get to where I felt genuine appreciation. I have been successful in doing this, and I know it can help many others who read through my memoir and then implement the daily activities provided for you in this book.

Having a gratitude journal has proven by research studies to be greatly beneficial in creating more abundance in many people's lives; it's a method of making a conscious decision to be happier and more grateful. When we take the time to write in a gratitude journal, we cultivate a powerful way of pulling ourselves out of autopilot mode! It has been said that for every positive compliment we receive, we remember four negative ones. Somehow, when we reflect, the negativity comes to the forefront, and that impacts how we view ourselves, our lives, and our future. Gratitude journals work to counteract that, erasing the negativity and pushing the spotlight onto the "highlight reel" of our lives, the stuff that really matters. We no longer just go through the motions when we choose to take a few minutes each day to mindfully reflect on the blessings that surround us. I started my gratitude journal by listing five things that I was thankful for, and I still stick to the number five, but I am now noticing more and beautiful things as they happen in the moment each day. I can truly say from personal experience that my gratitude journal changed my life, and I can't wait for you to see the same results that I have.

When we change our perspective of what we are going through, life takes on new meaning and we find our purpose, even when we are faced with great challenges. My wish for you as you read through the pages is that you will see how valuable you are, even on your hardest days.

Shannon

Memoir of a

Cancer Survivor

❤ Why Me? ❤

"What you perceive as failure today may actually be a crucial step towards the success you seek. Never give up."

- Richelle E. Goodrich, Smile Anyway

One of the sure ways to get stuck in a rut where we feel like we are lacking blessings in our lives is when we compare our lives with others who we perceive as more fortunate. When we compare our life to others' lives, this robs us of our own happiness. It's natural to make comparisons—we are hardwired to do so—and to set goals based on what others have achieved, but we need to be careful and take notice of what we already have that we are grateful for. If we strive each day to be better than we were yesterday, then this is a comparison that makes sense. When we set personal goals and do our daily best, this is more productive. We only have the ability to improve ourselves and then lead others by our example.

When I was sick in bed with cancer, friends or family would visit me and tell me that I inspired them; that they appreciated life more after watching what I was going through, trying to survive. Sometimes I thought, *You've got to be kidding me! How in the world do I inspire another while I am in pain and so incapacitated physically?* I was cynical and wondered if they would even say that to me if I wasn't sick. It's a very valid and important point. Our adversities give a glimpse to others of what they don't have to struggle with, and this shines a light in their own lives, bringing great insight to them to have gratitude for their health and even smaller things like walking across a room comfortably and sitting at the dinner table to eat with family or friends. Our adversities show others all that they have to be grateful for.

When the cancer spread to my bones and lungs, I was in a lot of pain. I thought to myself quite a few times, *Why me? Why is all of this happening to me? There were five kids in our family, and this is happening to me!* Looking back on my confusion and sour attitude back then, I realize I gained a brand new perspective on that question: *Why me?* One day the answer hit me hard and in an instant! The answer to that "poor, pitiful me mentality" was simple and founded on love. *If not me, then who else? I would never want anyone to take my place.* It shocks me to even imagine someone else going through what I have gone through. It would break my heart. I was glad it happened to me. I wouldn't want my children or siblings to go through it. I wouldn't want anyone I loved to have to fight for their life. I was in a crisis that was meant for me on my soul journey. How I grew from it and what attitude I had was going to be all up to me.

I can say with 100 percent certainty that I am grateful for all the adversity in my life. I actually appreciate it! I like the woman I have become over the years. There isn't any way to gain the knowledge I have acquired except through every challenge I pushed through. There are probably plenty of people who disagree with my perspective, but personally I am extremely grateful for all the adversities in my life. Most of the time we cannot see the good in something that has gone wrong until much later. We can lose a job or experience great hardship like losing our home or car. Later, we have new experiences as a direct result of these difficult ones—like finding a more fulfilling job, meeting new people, or seeing new places.

I have experienced this hundreds of times over the years. We can look at missed flights, traffic, or someone cancelling plans with us in a whole new way. We can still go through the emotions of feeling disappointment, but we can gain a new perspective that brings us new insight and keeps us going in a forward direction in life. We begin to see life's adversities as stepping stones rather than roadblocks. When we have a perspective of trying to find the blessings, it's like puzzle pieces falling into place as your life starts to spiral upward again. We begin to see how life brought us blessings through hardship. It can take days or decades to become aware of that.

With the attitude of gratitude as our mindset, it's easier to keep our focus on our own improvement, regardless of what happens to us. I had cancer twice and many other adversities physically and emotionally. I could easily give in to a negative attitude and believe a lie about myself that I am damaged and have less value because of going through serious health issues for so long. I could stay stuck in that attitude for quite a long time with a critical self-image that would only hurt me more over time. Or I could choose to acknowledge the blessings I still have around me and have an appreciation for new friends, doctors, and so much more who have helped me during all the tragedy in my life. I can look at all I have been through with more self-compassion and with a new purpose and see how life has new meaning to me now.

A final thought on appreciating adversity. I walked through the park in deep thought about my rough week. I shook my head frustrated about something I read,

"Appreciate Adversity in Life." I thought cynically, *How could anyone appreciate adversity?* Suddenly my foot was jabbed with pain from a sharp pebble that got lodged in my shoe. I took off my shoe to shake out the jagged intruder and felt the coolness of the grass caress my bare foot. I smiled with a new understanding and took off my other shoe.

♥ My Attitude Adjustment ♥

"Attitude is a little thing that makes a big difference."

~ Winston Churchill

When I had breast cancer and went through a bilateral mastectomy in October 2006, I did not do the recommended chemotherapy cocktail (three drugs) and I did not do the hormone therapy or radiation. I had experienced one complication after another. I was sick with staph twice after having surgery. The doctors then had to perform a corrective surgery, which required breaking my foot, and on top of that, I had two knee replacements. One knee replacement had complications; it was put in crooked, so I went through two more corrective surgeries. I had my gallbladder removed, uterine surgery, and other surgeries from the complications. I had 14 surgeries within two years, and it was very painful. The recovery time in between surgeries, looking back now, was not enough. It seemed like I had just started to ease into my recovery when I was back in the hospital having surgery yet again. My attitude during that period was not very good; I was terrified when it got to be about the seventh surgery. I was on antibiotics for months for a staph infection and was sick to my stomach. I was confined mostly to bed. Sometimes I would wake up very early in the morning because of the pain. I would take my medication and not be able to fall back to sleep, which meant I had a much longer day. It seemed like the time on the clock was in slow motion. In fact, time wasn't relevant except for doctor appointments. I found myself to be lonely and bored more often than not, but I did not want to be a burden on friends or my daughter.

I realize how depressing this sounds, but I was not happy. I needed help just getting to the bathroom, getting out of bed... I needed assistance for everything, even showering and washing my hair. I needed food in bed. I did not want to see my chest in the mirror because it was gone and there were hideous gashes for nine months before reconstructive surgery began. I desperately wanted to be able to get out of bed so that I could drive my car or go for a walk outside. I wanted to socialize with my friends. Now and then, I would snap back to reality and remember that there were people having to endure even greater struggles than myself, but I am ashamed to say I still felt my attitude headed in a downward spiral.

Somehow I reached a crossroads where I knew I needed to change my attitude. I was afraid of slipping into complete depression and knew if I continued feeling sorry for myself, I would never return to the positive, optimistic woman I used to be. I used to write in journals, and I had stopped doing that when I got sick with cancer. I remembered how I used to write five things I was grateful for and that there was a connection to feeling hopeful and abundant in life simply by being grateful for something no matter what adversity I was going through in my life. I knew it was time to start up a new gratitude journal. I looked around my bedroom to find things to be thankful for; you'd think being thankful to be alive would be enough, but I was still afraid and in my miserable frame of mind. Trust me, it wasn't easy to write five things in the beginning. I had to force myself to write, and my sloppy handwriting barely filled up a 1/4 page.

It read like this:

December 16th, 2006

Dear God,

1. *Thank you for my pillow.*

2. *Thank you for the air I am breathing.*

3. *Thank you for the soup. Even though it makes me sick, I know there are nutrients.*

4. *Thank you for my toothbrush.*

5. *Thank you for my son and daughter!*

My attitude did not change overnight. I was sad. I needed to forgive, apologize, and let go of resentment; it was definitely a process. I still felt cheated in life, not just from cancer, but also from my relationship, which had taken a huge hit. I missed my family. I felt my spirit diminishing. Believe me, you can do too much thinking when you are sick and confined to bed. There was a veil of despair separating me from everything good around me; I lost sight, but I was determined to reach happiness again. I always used to say, "If you don't feel like smiling, smile anyway because the rest of your body will eventually catch on."

I bought a beautiful journal and an assortment of colored pens to start this project. I wrote in my gratitude journal each day, and before long I was filling up an entire page each night. More time passed, and eventually I was filling up one or two pages. My handwriting was not sloppy anymore, and finally an attitude adjustment was taking place. It was getting to the point where I would feel concerned about leaving anything left unwritten that I was grateful for that day. I was grateful for the smallest things, like my soup spoon versus the regular teaspoons that caused more spills. I loved my flex straws for my protein drinks. I was grateful for phone calls from friends. We always laughed! I opened a letter one day, and inside there were drawings from my best friend's daughter. I used to hate the birds chirping outside my window each morning because they woke me up early, which meant a long day awake and stuck in bed. I began to notice my attitude changing; now I was grateful to hear them singing because they were a reminder for me that someday I was going to be free again. I just knew I would get through it all.

I took this attitude adjustment project a step further! I wrote down positive affirmations on pieces of paper. "You are loved," "There is beauty all around you," "God is with you," etc. I printed pictures of fairies and colored them in careful detail with pencils; they cheered me up! Their big beautiful wings signified freedom to me, and the long flowing hair and whimsical gowns signified femininity, which I had been so afraid of losing because of what I had lost with breast cancer. I had my daughter tape these positive affirmations on my ceiling for me, including each blade of my ceiling fan over my bed so I would wake up to a room with positive messages and start my day with a smile. I felt inspired and beautiful on the inside and felt I could get through just about anything, and my room reflected that.

What I have learned is this:

Sometimes we are given too much to handle, and each of us copes with it differently. Adversity showed me my abilities, and it shaped me into a strong and compassionate woman. It didn't happen overnight, and in some instances it would be years before I could look back at a burden I endured as something to be grateful for. What matters is I got to the point where I could have a fresh view of the situation. We all have the power of perception to see a lifetime of success and failures any way we wish. Some will see a life of many victories. Others will see many failures. Our attitude and our perception can constantly be adjusted. What we see is what we get.

To demonstrate what I mean, I will share a short story with a very powerful message.

"Once there were three bricklayers. When each bricklayer was approached and asked what he was doing, their responses were quite different. The first one answered gruffly, 'I'm laying bricks.' The second replied, 'I'm putting up a wall.' But the third bricklayer said with great pride, 'I'm building a cathedral.'"

The bricklayer story is a great reminder of how we can each have a different perspective of the same thing. Now when I am sick in bed, I have a different attitude. I can envision my body healing itself, and while I lay in bed resting, there is a whole lot of work going on inside my body by me being at peace and having an attitude of gratitude. Thank God I am alive and healing.

♥ Diagnosed: Breast Cancer ♥

"To have the courage to tell our story requires vulnerability and makes it easier for others to tell theirs."

- Shannon Knight

I was diagnosed with breast cancer on July 19, 2006, my brother's birthday.

At 4:30 p.m., Wednesday, July 19, 2006, my phone rang. It was the call I had patiently been waiting for since having the biopsy.

"Hello? Yes, this is Shannon. I'm fine, Nicole, thanks for asking. Oh good, you have my biopsy results. Please say it's good news!"

"What? Why does the doctor need to tell me the results in person? Is that normal? He wants to see me now?"

I lived all the way in the Tahuya Forest, in Mason County, Washington. At that time of the day, I knew there would be rush hour traffic. I would have to cross the Tacoma Narrows Bridge, and it would be at least a two-hour drive.

"I probably wouldn't get to your office until 6:30 or 7:00 p.m. Can I come in tomorrow morning, or could you please ask the doctor to give me my results over the phone?"

"He wants me to come now? What? Why do I need to bring a support person? Okay..." I hesitated. "Nicole, uh... should I be scared? I don't have a support person to be with me. Okay, fine, I'll just come alone. I'm on my way."

13

Many who have been diagnosed with cancer can probably relate to much of the phone conversation I had as I received the first hint of my diagnosis. The ride to the doctor's office was terrifying—I cried the entire way, gripping the steering wheel so tightly that my fingers ached. I found it difficult to concentrate on my driving, instead drifting off into fearful thoughts. I think angels must have been steering that day, because I do not recall one moment of that drive. I just remember that when I arrived, all I could see through the glass window was a light shining from the far corner of the medical office. Everything else was dark. It was after hours.

It felt eerie as Nicole escorted me through the dimly lit waiting area to the doctor's private office instead of the customary examining room. She put a box of Kleenex on his large cherrywood desk, within reach, and handed me a bottle of water decorated with a pink ribbon. My heart sank. This couldn't be good.

I'll never forget the moment I found out; I listened to my doctor without asking questions because I knew if I spoke a word, I would fall apart. Silence was my only strength in that moment—eerie silence, like the calm before the storm. My world was suddenly crashing down around me. I excused myself from the doctor's office, went to the restroom, put my hands on the sink, and looked in the mirror. I just whispered to myself over and over, "Not me!"

I had a bilateral mastectomy because of the location of the tumors. You think the scars are bad? Just imagine the emotional and mental pain that lingers long after the final antibiotic is digested. I got very sick after the surgery. I was bedridden and had a lot of time to do research on treatments. I chose to reject my doctor's suggestion of chemotherapy, radiation, and hormone therapy and instead decided to do several non-toxic therapies. Some people know that spicy food isn't for them, some people don't like flying on planes... I knew traditional medicine was not going to save me.

That day marked the start of when I found myself transported into a whole new way of life, awkwardly trying to figure out how to win my battle with cancer. I had no idea how to fight against an enemy I had seen do its worst to some of my relatives. I had Stage 3 breast cancer, my life was in danger, and the 1,100 miles that separate me from my family now felt like an abyss, stretching further into infinity than ever before.

I felt vulnerable and scared. I was a woman thrown into an unfamiliar arena to fight a battle of a magnitude I had never experienced before, and I knew nothing of the enemy. I transformed slowly, and it was painful. I learned that friends and family really cared, and they all had grand ideas as to how I should approach cancer treatment. I felt overwhelmed because my life depended on my choices. My strategy had to be successful because I was not willing to die from cancer!

I had a bilateral mastectomy. I was shocked by how I felt afterward. I was not prepared to feel as if I had just gone through an amputation. There had been no discussion, no preparation as to how much loss I would feel after surgery. Breasts are such a feminine attribute, and I had not realized the emotional pain I would experience once they were gone. I experienced complications from the surgery and became very ill with a staph infection. This complication lent me some time to learn about the world of alternative medicine for cancer.

I respect the reasons why people accept the therapies recommended by their conventional doctor. Often, a trusting doctor-patient relationship has been established in advance and that trust plays a role in decision making at a time when the patient is most terrified. A sense of urgency is conveyed by their physician and they respond accordingly, rushing to accept conventional treatment without pausing to discover what other healthier options are available.

I declined the standard recommended treatments of chemotherapy and radiation. Instead, I went to a small clinic in Arizona. There I received intravenous vitamin C and B-17, far-infrared sauna, and ultraviolet blood irradiation treatments.

♥ Cowboy Angel ♥

"Cowboys and angels, leather and lace
Salt of the Earth meets heavenly grace
Cowboys and angels, tested and tried
It's a long way to heaven
And one heck of a ride"

-Unknown

When I was fighting cancer the first time, I made new friends. My life was changing dramatically, and I will be forever grateful to the people who came in to my life and gave their love and support so freely. Time is a funny thing sometimes when it comes to how long it takes to connect. When you meet someone fighting for their life at the same time you are, there is an instant bond.

We were both in the cancer war zone; we knew life was precious. Not many people have heard about the man I met at a holistic healing center for cancer in Arizona. The clinic is no longer there, but I have the memory of it.

I will just call him Angel in my story. Angel lost his battle, and it just feels improper to mention his real name. I will be forever grateful to Angel, and I know I will never forget him. He made a positive impact in my life while I battled stage 3 breast cancer and other hardships, such as a boyfriend cheating on me during that time. I went through many surgeries. I had a lot of pain in my heart and my body.

We met in the Spring of 2007. Angel was nearing the end of battling Stage 4 cancer unsuccessfully while I was heading towards victory. My body hurt everywhere from all the previous surgeries and especially the most recent one, which was a corrective knee replacement surgery. I still had 25 stitches in my knee when I took that trip to Arizona. Getting there was hell because my flight was delayed! I sat in the Seattle airport for several hours because of bad weather. It was only days following my knee surgery, and my pain medication was packed away in my luggage already checked in for my flight. I cried from the excruciating pain; I had three screws in my knee and had to keep my knee straight. What was I thinking, traveling like this! Well, I've always been strong willed, and I wanted to live, so I did not let that surgery stop me from traveling to a little clinic that would boost my immune system with holistic treatments. I wanted to live.

I finally arrived in Arizona and went to the clinic the following morning. My pain was not manageable yet, and I did not want to talk to any of the other patients. I didn't feel well and was not in the mood to talk to the other patients. It took me a while to trust and open up

Angel was one of the five patients there receiving treatment. He was a rugged cowboy with a horse ranch in Wyoming. He had been through hell and back with chemotherapy more than once and suffered from neuropathy from the side effects of chemotherapy. He had numbness in his feet and hands and walked off balance because of it. I learned from the clinic staff that Angel did not talk much to anyone. I just laid down, hurting, with stitches in my leg and a broken heart from my boyfriend cheating—and dealing with the fear of stage 3 cancer. I was emotionally and physically a wreck. I was also mourning the loss of my aunt who had lost her battle to cancer the week before I set out to Arizona. I was sad and broken inside and out.

About one week into treatment, Angel and I sat outside on the patio as usual in the desert morning sun. Our chairs were about 15 feet apart from each other. It was a beautiful morning to be soaking up the rays and getting some vitamin D. I was writing in my journal like I normally did and keeping to myself. We never talked until this one morning. He broke the silence and finally spoke to me. He said, "So what do you write in that little book of yours?" I was writing everything I was feeling about my experience there. I answered him and told him it was just a personal journal. That is how our friendship started. After about an hour of yelling back and forth to one another, attempting to have a conversation with the distance of our chairs being so far from each other, we both laughed, and he asked, "Do you mind if I bring my chair closer?" I said that it would make it easier to for us to talk. So, that's what he did, and our friendship began.

We talked with one another about things we didn't talk about with our family and friends; we were straightforward with each other. We had the common connection that made it easier. He was kind, smart, and a little stoic with everyone else.

One morning, about two weeks into our cancer treatments, I became focused on a winding staircase outside in the back of the building that went up to the rooftop. I hobbled over there with my walker and stood there looking up. I hung onto the railing of the stairs, thinking about the past and daydreaming about the future. I wanted to climb those stairs so bad. I knew they led up to a patio or roof. I wanted to be alone up there and see the desert.

Angel's rugged voice snapped me suddenly out of my thoughts. He yelled out to me, "Damn, woman! Are you crazy? You want to go up those stairs with your leg like that? Don't even think about doing that alone!"

I said, "Well, I do want to, but I won't!" I told him that I wished I could get up there to see the desert from up high. There was a liberating feeling I got from imagining this. I wanted just a moment to feel like that.

He hobbled up from his chair. He staggered when he walked. In spite of the numbing in his feet, he was eager to help me. Together, we slowly did the climb up those stairs. It hurt, and I didn't care. We did it! The view was worth the climb! The desert was so vast and beautiful in its unique way. The Sonora cactus and prickly bushes had a harsh beauty all across the desert. Seeing the orange wildflowers that managed to blossom in such rugged terrain gave me hope. If a delicate flower could bloom under the harshest of conditions, maybe I could too!

I had traveled far, leaving the green lushness of Seattle. Its little moments like that which can transcend you and restore a diminished spirit. I felt taller, freer, and more capable just by breathing in the view of a new kind of beauty.

I thought about Angel a lot during those days. A real cowboy with a ranch in Wyoming. He said he had 120 horses and that one day, when I got well, I could come out and learn to ride. He was just a bit younger than my father, and I was glad I could make him laugh. I knew he was very sick and did not think he was going to conquer cancer after hearing about his long journey. He was very sick.

I was going to fly home and really missed my kids. My daughter lived in Las Vegas, which was not far from where I was at, considering my home was Seattle. Angel knew I missed them. I especially missed my daughter at this time because she had been having a rough time. Angel told me he felt like his time was running out and that he wanted to have one last visit with some friends of his in Las Vegas. He said, "You need to take a break. Let me drive you to Las Vegas to see your daughter."

The visual of us together was comical but I agreed anyway. I had been dependent on a walker from the knee surgery and could not put weight on my leg because of the pins in my knee. He insisted on walking without the cane he usually used and stumbled a lot.

His plan was a good one because he was happy. I knew I would be too. When we got to Las Vegas, he pushed me in a wheelchair through a casino, and I knew he was using the wheelchair to stabilize himself a bit. I worried about him, but he said, "You can't walk, and I want you with me because you make me laugh." How could I complain? I spent a day with him like that.

He talked about life and death, and I became quiet. I didn't want to think about death. He was coming to terms with his end of life, and I wanted nothing to do with the subject! He talked about his sister and his hometown. I couldn't see how many times he stumbled behind me as he pushed me around in the wheelchair, but I know he did. He laughed and said to me, "Now see, isn't this better than going back to Washington and dealing with a bad break-up!" You need to laugh, girl. I did laugh, and he was right. I worried about him overexerting himself, but there wasn't a thing I could do about it. I was out of my element, and it was good for me because there were only two other people that knew how to do that with me. My best friend and my daughter. We were laughing a lot now, and for that time, we were alive! I was so thankful for the escape.

I just have so many stories I could tell about friends who became family, and Angel became my family. It is trust built on mutual empathy and compassion. I trusted him, and I know it was mutual. When I think about our time and the raw conversation of what he was facing, I get tears. Here was a man I had the honor of knowing for a short while.

I never saw Angel again after that day in Las Vegas. He is with the angels now, probably surrounded by horses. I found out when I was home and getting ready to mail him a thank you letter and picture of me. I only had his phone number and did not have his address. He had a landline at the ranch and his cell phone. In a flash, I remembered something that said when we had said goodbye. Angel said if I ever tried to call him and his phone was disconnected, that meant he had finally gone to meet his maker. I tried his cell phone first. The line was disconnected. My hands were shaking as I dialed the landline number of his ranch phone. I just heard a disconnect recording.

In our last conversation, I asked Angel if I could visit him, and he said no. He said it was because he wanted me just to remember the good times in Arizona and Las Vegas. I was beginning to realize that it was about the time he was nearing his final weeks. I didn't want to believe he was gone, so I called around, and I confirmed it later that he was gone. The short time and memories together flooded me. I may not have known about Angel's whole life, but I know he "loved." I experienced his courage. I experienced him defending me at one point and saw that he was not a quitter. He accepted "what was" like a gentleman, and he just amazed me!

Angel had dignity. He never criticized me, and he always lifted me up. He always talked to me as if his messages were something he never wanted me to forget. It meant everything to him that I understood his words. He explained to me my value and told me to remember his words. He said it was my determination and strength that would save my life, and he said, "Your strength and forthrightness will be intimidating to men." He told me not to take that the wrong way and that it was better to be wise and strong instead of stupid and broken.

He said," You are going to live a healthy happy life and love again. So promise me you won't settle for bullsh*t from guys! He said, "Promise me, Shannon! These men know what they are doing and pretend that they don't." He told me to take care of myself.

So now I understand what he was trying to say. I believe we meet people for a reason. Angel knew I had a boyfriend who was not faithful to me during my battle, as we kept talking day after day. When I finally told him my boyfriend's name and that he was from Wyoming, he mentioned he was also from Wyoming. The craziest thing was that Angel knew my boyfriend's family. He had gone to school with my boyfriend's mother. We both just about fell out of our seats when we discovered this. I was from Seattle; he was from Wyoming. We both traveled so far to Arizona to try and heal. There were only five patients total.

Angel, I still hear your solid cowboy advice! I will never give up that softer side of me, but I have wizened up. It does take a while! I will stay the way I am for the most part, but I have learned to keep my eyes wide open. Your picture with me in the desert on our last day there is a reminder to stay true to myself. We covered some new ground in our conversations, and we had a change of perspective on many issues concerning life and death.

Since our last days together, I have arrived at many crossroads in my life where things like this have happened to me. I think of the coincidence of meeting and how God brings people together for our soul's growth. I am an optimist, and we can learn or complain. Angel, you were a change angel for me. The memories are what kept me going on the right path all my life. I am ready for life's next lesson, and I know it does not have to mean a break-up or be at the expense of me having a broken heart. I want to keep growing in love and compassion. I never question why my life was hard because we can always be in 100 percent more difficult circumstances if we dare to think about it. I say, let's count our blessings and just work through it, hang onto integrity, and try to get a new perspective. After all, it's the only thing any of us have real control over.

Angel, you were right. I'm different, quirky as you put it. Some people don't get me, and I don't mind it anymore because my path is much clearer and it takes a unique person to lead. I don't want to be like everyone else. I want to be different, authentic, and embrace all of who I am.

RIP my dear friend; I will see you later, much later, Cowboy Angel.

♥ Letting Go of Pride ♥

"Pride is your greatest enemy; humility is your greatest friend."

- John R.W. Stott

I have always had trouble reaching out and asking for help. I never wanted to be a burden or inconvenience anyone. Pride got in the way of letting people see that I needed help or wasn't capable of doing something on my own. When I needed help and did not reach out, it almost always got to a point where I would have to ask for help anyway because I would make matters worse. I remember one incident with my best friend, Heather. I had no family in WA; I had nowhere to go. My friends were my family. I was sick with stage 3 cancer, and I didn't have a good leg to stand on—literally! I had bilateral knee replacements, but one knee had to get a second and third operation because of complications. I had been through a bilateral mastectomy and had complications with a staph infection. I had several more surgeries, and the pain was constant from October 2006 until New Year's Day in 2008.

The worst pain of all was my shattered heart. My boyfriend was unfaithful for about a year. My heart was broken into pieces, so there were more than physical wounds. I felt like I had slipped off of a trapeze bar and there was no one there to catch me and, worst of all, no net below. The truth is when we hide and refuse to let someone see us fall, we are choosing to have the net our friends carry for each other removed. We want to hide our wounds and our shortcomings at the complete risk of not getting any help and spiraling even further down.

My stubborn, foolish pride was the only reason they were not there for me because I kept pushing people out. I didn't want people to see all the mess because my self-esteem had crashed and I judged myself so harshly. I had very little self-compassion back then.

I finally got so broke down and worn out that it forced me to muster up the courage to get out of my own way and call Heather. My heart was the most fragile part of my body, and the pain of a broken heart hurt far worse than any of the physical challenges of cancer, surgeries, or infection. I remember New Year's Day when I finally hit rock bottom and found out that morning my boyfriend was unfaithful. I lived with him, and he was the one taking care of me, so I was confused. Who would take his place where I would not be a burden? I did not want to add stress to the lives of the people I loved.

I will always remember Heather's words on the phone when I called her that morning asking for help and for her to come get me. She said, "I've been waiting for you to ask me for help, baby! Will I be coming to your house with boxes for packing you up and getting you out, or will we be packing a suitcase for a short visit? I took in a long slow breath encapsulating the words I was afraid to say to her. I heard her say again, "Shannon, will we be needing boxes or a suitcase?"

I broke the silence with a whisper, "Boxes...?" Heather replied, "You don't sound sure, honey. You know me; I will show up with boxes and have you packed up and out of there in no time!"

I said, "I'm sure. Boxes."

Why was I so embarrassed and scared to be transparent with her about the mess I got myself into?

It wasn't like she couldn't see all that had transpired over the last year. She always had words of wisdom that I would ignore because of my stubbornness and desire to try and make something good out of something completely wrong for me.

She replied instantly, "Alright, say no more; we're on our way!"

I apologized for being a burden, especially since I could not physically pack a single thing.

She was very quick to set me straight. She laughed and said, "Sweetie, that's what friends are for!" We will be a burden to each other sometimes, and when you have real friends, they will be there for you and want to help ease it for you. Then she laughed again and said, "Just you wait. I'm going to need you someday!

She and her husband then showed up, and they packed my stuff and had me out of my house and in the driveway of her home by midnight. I was so afraid to take her up on an offer of moving in with them numerous times. She watched me continually struggling. It was like watching me swim upstream in a river carrying way too many burdens on my back. This time I was too tired and began sinking. I surrendered. It took me nine months, but I finally surrendered to true friendship.

When we pulled into the driveway of her house, it was raining gently, and I started crying from fear, relief, and just not knowing where I belonged. I challenged her once again with my stubbornness as we sat in the car talking things through, this time just trying to get me through my emotionally broken state. I still did not want to be a burden. Next, Heather's face lit up as she smiled with a brilliant idea to get me to say what I wanted for myself. She said the cutest thing to me. God, how I love her playfulness when she is also actually being serious. I am sure no one will ever say something like this to me ever again. She asked me, "Shannon, if you were a princess and could have whatever you wanted...if you could live wherever you wanted right now, and it was not a problem in spite of what you think, where would you live?"

In a flash, I knew the answer, but I said, "I'm afraid to tell you because it's not possible, I know what I want though."

She said, "Dammit, go with it! I said you are a princess and you can have whatever you want!"

I laughed and cried at the same time and finally got the words out. I said, "I would want to stay here with you and your family because I feel safe and loved by all of you, but where would I fit?"

She said, "Fine, now was that so hard? Wish granted!"

In a day she transformed her living room into a bedroom for me. She even pulled out a queen size bed from the garage and set it up for me in the living room. I was moved and humbled by the true meaning of friendship. The gratitude I felt was immeasurable, and I felt loved every day. Our adversities can bring out so many attributes in people who love us if we let them. I will forever be grateful to her and her family.

During that prior year, I had my list of reasons that made sense to me, but looking back they were prideful reasons and all fear based. I had been hurt so much in my past that I was sure that some form of regret would come from allowing my dearest friend to help me. I had to trust, and I had to let go in this extreme time of adversity. This is a big reason people sink with their pride. I am a woman who has been through that sinking in deep waters! There was a ball and chain wrapped around my ankle with five letters painted on it, "PRIDE".

I was blessed to see more of my friends come in and help. When Heather and her family moved to Redding, CA due to a job promotion, I was still healing and had trouble walking. We had another friend in our group, Melody, who was getting ready to get married and certainly had a full plate of things to do. She and her fiancé immediately opened their home to me. I was given a guest room and felt the feeling of real friendship yet again. My cup had indeed runneth over with gratitude. How can so many people be so loving and giving? I remember hobbling around in a walker, trying to do some light chores around the house to show some appreciation, and one day, I went to my bedroom, and there was a single envelope resting on my pillow. The words were kind and direct. She wrote that she was happy to have me in their home and that she hoped I would feel comfortable there. She hoped we would become closer during this time. She wanted me to know she felt a kindredness like sisters. She even signed it, "Your sister, Melody."

Later that evening, Melody knocked on my bedroom door, and I hugged her and thanked her for the beautiful card. She said, "You're welcome," and then asked me something I will never forget. She said, "Shannon, can you do me a favor?"

I said, "Sure, what?"

She said, "Can you please relax in our home like a family member? We don't need you to try and pay us back by cleaning our house while we are at work. We appreciate the gesture, but we asked you to stay with us in our house because we love you and hope you will feel like part of our family. We want you to just relax in our home. We don't need you to pay rent; we've handled our mortgage and bills just fine long before we invited you here, and we will continue to do so. We want you to feel at home, and it would really make us happy if you would just accept staying here as a gift from us to you to help make your life more comfortable. Can you do that?"

I nodded with tears running down my face, a little embarrassed but feeling very loved and so grateful. I thanked her, and I knew she meant every word. It is not easy to receive. It is the strangest thing to be able to give and have a tough time receiving. I am learning that this is a gift we give to others.

♥ *Hurricane Wilma* ♥

"Storms draw something out of us that calm seas don't."

- Bill Hybels

Prior to being diagnosed with cancer, I had experienced and witnessed other kinds of adversity. I had traveled to Cozumel, MX with a group of friends to celebrate a wedding. It was October 2005, and we were having the time of our lives. I was laying on the beach, soaking up the sun, when two of my friends walked over to let me know we had a hurricane heading our way. I had never been in a hurricane before and did not know what to expect. I was from Southern California and had been in some pretty big earthquakes over the course of my life. I followed the resort staff's instructions and grabbed only my pillow, passport, purse, and phone. We had to leave everything in our rooms. On October 19th, Hurricane Wilma made landfall on the small island of Cozumel. It broke the record books as it reached its peak intensity.

Hurricane Wilma had the smallest eye on record when it reached a diameter of only 3.2 km (2 mi) on October 19. This tiny eye was replaced with a second much larger eye, 64-97 km (40-60 mi) in diameter. I was terrified. When I went back to my hotel room, there was glass everywhere and everything was underwater. My room was facing the ocean front, so the sliding glass door was taken out completely. I was terrified.

I remember sleeping on a wet mattress and having no plumbing for the week that followed. It was surreal. At night I could hear large crabs walking across the hotel floor, their claws clacking on the tile. My anxiety level was high. The airport was underwater, so I would not be flying home. The resort staff was so humble and accommodating while they were having to rebuild their homes. Many victims were injured and bleeding, and some families were in their cars. I remember the local people sleeping on stairs.

In the middle of such adversity in Cozumel, I saw smiles and kindness demonstrated constantly to me and all the other tourists. I learned a lot about community while I was there. I saw humility and kindness.

I needed to find a landline somewhere to call my family and my place of employment. Someone told me about a phone on the eleventh floor, so I made my way there; the water was ankle deep. The phone on the wall reminded me of the phone I grew up with. It was on our kitchen wall, and all seven of us shared it. The first person I called was my mother, and it felt so good to hear her voice. I wanted to get home; the conditions were so sad and heart wrenching.

Nervously, I made my calls, standing in the water. Paper was floating around, and for an instant, a scene from the movie *Titanic*, where the cabin was filling up with water, flashed into my mind. There was a dragging feeling as I walked through the office. I wondered how all the water got in on the 11th floor.

When I made my calls, I had learned that my son had a stroke. I felt helpless and couldn't understand how all this could be happening at once. You really get a sense of all you have to be thankful for when the world seems to be falling apart around you. I couldn't wait to see my kids again. *Will my son be alright?* I was stuck!

I climbed up to the rooftop to get a look of the island. The power of the hurricane was massive and had affected every structure in Cozumel. Trees and power lines were knocked down, and everywhere I looked was complete devastation. I saw what used to be an airport underwater and had heard that no flights would be coming in to take us home. *How could everything change overnight like this? How will they ever rebuild? How will they survive without tourists being able to visit?* All the store fronts were destroyed, and much of the merchandise washed out to sea.

I remember how I couldn't wait to get home to the common luxuries I took for granted, like clean water, dry clothes, and plumbing.

A cruise liner showed up to deliver water, beans, rice, diapers, and other necessities. There were 80 Americans that would be going home on that ship. There was more staff on that ship than there were passengers. I remember the warmth of the water on my skin after weeks of no shower. I remember the coolness of the sheets and the dry mattress. I fell asleep quickly, and I remember when I woke up to the sound of a man's voice on the intercom announcing an incredible buffet laid out for us. I remember the comforting words and sentiments expressed to us. When I saw all the food laid out before us, I couldn't help but feel like Shirley temple in the movie *The Little Princess*. She awoke one day to a feast after staying in a cold uncomfortable basement.

I arrived back home to Seattle, WA on October 31st. I was gone a total of 16 days. I was like a kid when I got home; I ran around the house, thanking my curtains that provide privacy and showering appreciation on my comfy bed and dry towels. Everything in my path seemed brand new to me. It is through adversity where we realize all that we have that we take for granted.

When I got home and was able to see my son and daughter, I realized how delicate life was and how time is not guaranteed. I learned that at any given moment something unpredictable can happen and that life is precious. I wanted to teach them that no matter what happens, our family is important. We should always be grateful we have each other and make sure the final words we say are loving words. We are not promised tomorrow, and the memories we make each day are all that we leave behind.

As for my friends and the rest of my family, they were interested in the adventure of it all but mostly glad I was alright. I am sure they had memories of the giant California earthquakes we all feared through together. We have been through many and expressed our gratefulness to all be safe during those times.

♥ Big Family in a Small House ♥

"Having a large family is a lot of things; it's chaos and frustration or an anchor in stormy waters. Sometimes rocky yet sometimes the greatest comfort. It's an unconditional love I will never take for granted."

~ Shannon Knight

I grew up with four brothers and sisters and very humble beginnings. My twin sister and I had dresser drawers for a bed when we were babies. Four of us kids were in diapers at the same time, and my parents could not afford a washing machine. My slender, 5'6" mother would manage to take all of us to the laundromat to do the laundry.

When we were older, I remember mattresses on the floor for beds and lots of chores. We all got plenty to eat; but, if we wanted more and there was no more to eat, Mom would say, "No, honey, you got plenty. We need to save some for your father when he gets home! Dad was 6'4" and ate a lot. In all, we were a family of seven (five kids in an apartment on Saticoy in Canoga Park, CA). In 1978, we moved to a house in Simi Valley CA. I still shared a room until I turned 18.

Meals were modest and filled our bellies. Breakfast was oatmeal or cream of wheat, and on the weekend we'd sometimes have eggs or pancakes. Lunch was bologna and American cheese sandwiches, peanut butter and jelly, and Kool-Aid. Our dinners were delicious because it was either Mexican or Italian much of the time. Mom could cook creatively on such a tight budget. She would make a big pot of beans and rice or spaghetti, which would last a few days for all of us!

For Christmas 2017, my mother gave me the cookbook she got as a wedding present. It's a red and white checkered Betty Crocker three-ring binder. It's a year older than me! My mother used that book, and so did I! We loved the food we ate, and we learned to cook at a young age as well.

Mom was handy with her tan colored Singer sewing machine and saved money by making our clothing and even outfits for our dolls! She taught us how to use that thing! The three of us girls had to share a closet at times and learned to share our clothes through high school.

We had a blast playing outside—kick the can or learning new dances in the street. When the street lights went on, we knew to high-tail home! Our family enjoyed playing card games like Hearts, Canasta, and Rummy. We also played board games like Parcheesi and Monopoly, and we loved playing charades. Watching everyone acting in silence so we could guess was hilarious! That's what was great about living in a small home and having a big family. We had teams! If we wanted to ride a bike, we rode mom's bicycle, which had a baby seat on the back. We shared one pair of roller skates for a while until they could afford skates for each of us one Christmas.

Our neighborhood kids became like family to us. We were creative! We would pack lunches and walk to the nearby park and hang out with friends. We shared one phone and only were allowed 15 minutes to talk to a friend! That's it; not a minute longer. We did not have call waiting so, if someone tried to call, it was a busy signal. Mom needed the phone to be free in case Dad needed something.

We fought! Boy did we fight! We had to make pacts, keep secrets, and if we were going to do something like sneak out a window, you had to get an agreement from every sibling, not to tell; this taught us strategy. I know you think it's terrible, but it did!

After every argument, my mom would tell us that we'd be each other's best friends someday, which we would naturally balk at for being impossible. Of course, she was right! At least to some degree. It's like we survived a war together. When we recount stories with each other, we laugh at things we thought were so seriously wrong at the time. I am so grateful for my siblings. I don't talk to my brothers often, but I love them immensely. I talk to my sisters quite often.

I told my parents that they should be proud that they raised children who are problem solvers, self-starters, and not afraid to start their own businesses. I said to them that because of our upbringing we are creative and excited about starting something on our own. We are not followers, and they taught us values. We lead at what we do with confidence because they instilled that in all of us.

When we were old enough to work, we contributed a third of our paycheck to the household to help pay for food, clothing, and utilities. We walked everywhere to fill out applications, and we accepted the position if we got it. We didn't sit around declining jobs, looking for that perfect one. It was humbling and a good learning experience for us. We worked hard and never said we were going to quit if things displeased us. We respected our boss and would only leave a job if we had secured another place of employment. Our friends never made fun of where we worked. We were happy for each other in my neighborhood if we got work. I am so grateful for that lesson! It just made me want to work harder and be creative in getting money to get out on my own. We learned about contribution and not being entitled to anything.

We knew better than to sass or argue with our parents! We would get grounded! We respected them and knew the boundaries we were not to cross. I cannot tell you how many fights my brothers, sisters, and I got into while we were growing up. Things could get pretty rough when we were at our worst, but we managed to avoid having to be rushed to the hospital. We had family meetings to discuss our behavior.

My parents could not afford to put us through college or buy us high school yearbooks. What they did have for us were books! We could read the encyclopedia and the National Geographic collection. I remember my Nancy Drew collection. I loved solving mysteries. My parents' budget was tight. Some Christmases were just a doll and a stocking filled with nuts and Christmas candy. I still have a ragdoll—I call her my "Heather Doll"—and it will always be a reminder of my humble beginnings and how we are brought up to appreciate the small things. It has made a big difference in my own adult life. It taught me about perseverance and never giving up.

We did not complain to our parents about what we thought we should have because our friends had something. We were happy with every gift we got! Our parents taught us things that helped us to be independent and strategize. We walked to our jobs, even on the sweltering days in August. Dad had the car and needed it to drive to work. We knew walking was what we had to do.

I remember the Christmas dance skits and plays we would do for Dad. Mom was the director, and we couldn't wait to show Dad! She also started a dance group called the Sweethearts where my sisters and I belonged to with two other girlfriends. There were five of us, and we would perform at schools.

I remember forming a club with my sisters and friends. There was a membership, and we cleaned out an old storage shed that had been sitting in the backyard of my friend Stacy's house. It had rotted potatoes in it and spiderwebs. We cleaned it for days and added curtains. We found ways to make money! I directed a play for the kids in the neighborhood, and we sold lemonade. We turned Stacy's driveway into a skating rink and charged a nickel. It was the only one on our block that had brand new concrete instead of cracked, bumpy asphalt from the earthquakes; a prime location to skate!

When you grow up with a lot of friends and in a crowded small house, you learn that close families have to work out things. You cannot isolate yourself and play video games all day alone in your room. You are always planning things.

I love my memories and my family, and most of all I am grateful for being a big family in a small house! Even though we move on as adults, get caught up in our own lives, having our own children and grandchildren, I know that we love each other. My family is the most valuable thing in the world, and they have marked my heart forever.

♥ Cancer Runs in My Family ♥

"Love is life. And if you miss love, you miss life."

- Leo Buscaglia

I have witnessed many cancer battles in my life. As far back as when I was a young girl, and even through my teenage years, my grandma always looked well. She was strong, compassionate, and wise. She had the most beautiful brown eyes, and I never saw her get upset once in my life. If she wore makeup at all, it was minimal. She had a natural beauty. I never saw her complain. She made the most delicious peanut butter and banana sandwiches, and her cooking was scrumptious! She had a way of getting us kids to do things like going outside as if it was the greatest idea ever! There were a lot of grandchildren, and she just knew how to handle us. She was a very good listener with a gentle heart. To me, she was the kind of woman who had vitality. She was an artist, and I remember how much I loved her drawings and paintings.

Then, when I was only 23 years old, she became sick with cancer. She didn't even complain then! She lost weight and started wearing a wig. I thought she had lost her hair because of the cancer, but I later learned it was the chemotherapy that had caused her hair loss.

She wasn't the only one. Both my grandfathers died of cancer, and then one of my aunts got cancer, underwent chemotherapy, and died. Understandably, I was afraid of cancer and chemotherapy. From my perspective, if you got cancer, you were going to suffer from the treatment more than the disease, and even then... there was absolutely no guarantee you were going to beat it.

As a life coach, I am passionate about helping people with cancer because I have personally battled it twice and so many family members, who I love so dearly, have had to battle it as well! I have 14 close family members who have battled cancer since 1988. Every one of us took a different approach to try and survive. We had to choose a way to heal that felt right for us. These decisions are never easy, especially with so much conflicting information available on the internet today. I respect each journey, and I understand how it feels. It's like being drafted to fight in a war you never even saw coming.

Healing your body from cancer requires trying different methods sometimes. You can try conventional, find out your body is not responding to the treatment, and then try another drug. There are all kinds of trial drug studies. You could do something new, like alternative cancer treatment, after all conventional avenues have been exhausted. Some have tried the conventional arsenal of chemo, surgery, or radiation with success, and even though they dealt with very harsh side effects, they still had success and never saw cancer return. There are also survivors who did not have a long-lasting response from conventional medicine and had a recurrence of metastatic disease, stage 3 or 4; this is when people typically become open to looking at alternative treatments.

No treatment for any disease brings a promise of healing. It is not easy figuring out how to save your life. My family did various treatments all across the board. Some chose chemo, others radiation, some surgery, some integrative, and some chose a holistic approach. Each chose different diets; some even tried more than one. There are numerous dietary theories for cancer, not counting thousands of supplements. And you know what I have learned? It's different for everyone.

I am just grateful that my family has all had such a positive attitude while fighting. I think cancer is a call to action on all fronts of our lives. We slow down and take less for granted. When I talk to my family, some of the things they say are such an inspiration. We have become softer with our opinions, in many ways, because we have experienced cancer from many different perspectives. We have chosen various forms of treatment, some more debilitating than others, but we love each other regardless of our differences. That's real love. The heart must be a part of this journey the whole way through! When we love our family and see that they are scared and doing their best, we support and love them, no matter what!

I love my family, and if a family member of mine is diagnosed with cancer. I support their choice regardless of what I did. Whoever gives their advice will not be the one experiencing the results of their choice. You decide what goes into your body. You deserve to be loved and supported through the most difficult time of having to make vital decisions.

The list below is my family members affected by cancer.

- Myself: Stage 4 – Alternative – success
- Myself: Stage 3 – Surgery/no chemo – unsuccessful
- My Twin Sister: Alternative and surgery – success
- My Son: Surgery at age 9 for skin cancer – success
- Grandpa, Mom's side: Conventional – unsuccessful
- Uncle, Mom's side: Conventional – success

- Uncle, Mom's side: Conventional – success
- Uncle, Mom's side: Integrative – success
- Aunt, Mom's side: Conventional – success
- Aunt, Mom's side: Conventional – success
- Aunt, Mom's side: Conventional – success
- Cousin, Mom's side: Conventional – unsuccessful
- Grandma, Dad's side: Chemo – unsuccessful
- Grandpa, Dad's side: Conventional – unsuccessful
- Aunt, Dad's side: Conventional – unsuccessful

♥ Beating Stage 4 Breast Cancer ♥

How can I wake up without smiling and being grateful for the very breath I take as I start thinking about what blessings today might bring?

- Shannon Knight

There has been no greater feeling in the world for me than my doctor telling me that I beat stage 3 breast cancer! I'll never forget that day of my appointment. I sat in the UW Medical Center waiting room anticipating good news from my labs. Many people sat in the waiting room with their loved ones. I could tell which had been doing chemo and radiation because they looked weak, scared, and sick. I stared out the big glass window and thought how strange it was to see snow on the ground in April. It felt pure and new and gave me such a good feeling in that waiting room. I prayed the whole time until they called my name. I sat and waited for my results and had tears of joy when I got the results that I was cancer free. I wanted to hug my family and friends, but I had gone to that appointment alone. Finally, I was cancer free!

I was symptom free for a year and a half, and during that time, I felt relief and excited about getting on with a normal life. It was August 2009 when I left the cloudy state of Washington and moved back to sunny Southern California. I was so excited to start life over and put cancer behind me. I looked forward to seeing my family and friends.

Around the holiday season, I started developing a chronic cough and was diagnosed with asthma. I made several trips to the doctor and emergency room because it was getting increasingly worse, and I was diagnosed with costochondritis, as well, and pain began to develop on my sternum. Eventually my primary care physician saw a lump developing on my sternum, and she recommended I see an oncologist to have it checked out.

In July 2010, I got results back from a biopsy that confirmed my worst fear. I had a recurrence of stage 4 breast cancer with metastasis to my lymph nodes, ribs, clavicle, lungs, and sternum. I would have to fight for my life a second time. My UCLA doctor recommended conventional treatments, and once again, I knew I wanted to find a healthier option to get well.

I agreed to radiation treatments on my sternum to stop a tumor from paralyzing me, but again, I refused chemo, as I knew by then that my immune system just wouldn't take it. My physician did all he was allowed to do, but his best was not enough. When I walked out of his office after his discouraging words—"There is nothing left we can do for you"—I was devastated. He had given me three months to a year to live and when you hear something like that it knocks the wind out of you.

After the shock wore off, and some deep personal introspection, I picked myself up. I didn't waste any time—I didn't have any time to waste! Literally, there was no time to mess around with juices or changing my diet. I was under the gun. I researched advanced yet non-toxic therapies, ones that wouldn't hurt me... and I knew I had to get out of the country to get them.

My amazing friends in Seattle held a fundraiser, which raised enough money to get me to CMN hospital in Mexico for the alternative cancer treatments I wanted. This hospital has been offering hope to cancer patients for over 30 years. In the 12 days I was there, I didn't leave the hospital. I received dendritic cell therapy, ozone therapy, B17 and vitamin C IVs, enzymes, ultraviolet light, far infrared, hyperbaric oxygen, UBI, and many other therapies. There are so many treatments that can restore the immune system, destroy cancer, and gently detoxify harmful pathogens, which was crucial for me. Later, I went back and received the autologous bone marrow stem cell transplant, which is now included in the treatment protocol. With these non-toxic treatments, I started to feel better, even while I was still in the hospital, instead of feeling worse, which is what happens with conventional treatments.

A cancer diagnosis seems to be the end of the road. After a long, hard battle, the oncologist says, "There is nothing left we can do for you." The patient is in shock; she goes home feeling scared and tells her loved ones that the oncologist said, "It's over." Getting one's affairs in order can mean anything. For me, it meant fundraising and getting ready for CMN Hospital in Mexico. It doesn't matter what the doctors tell us. There are no guarantees in this life, so how can anyone give up when they have the will to survive?

The type of cancer I battled in 2010 has a 1% survival rate, and now I'm healthy and on a life mission to help others who don't want to give up. There is hope! For me, it was worth the fight do be able to do what I am doing now.

One of the most common questions a cancer patient asks a cancer treatment facility is, "What is the survival rate?" Imagine what would happen if a doctor turned that question around on her patients and asked what they thought their survival rates were? If she asked them what their plans were in this healing partnership?

Patients do have choices about how they treat their bodies.

I remember when I first met my oncologist and we were discussing my treatment options. He terrified me with the mortality rate! We are brainwashed to be afraid of leaving our country for treatment and healing. We are taught to think hospitals in Mexico are dirty and dangerous. I went to Mexico so I could use therapies that the United States won't approve just because drug companies cannot put patents on them. Just because a treatment is not FDA approved does not mean it doesn't work. I did not get sick with my cancer therapies. I did not vomit or lose my hair, and I was cured in eight months.

My healing was not a miracle; surviving the barbaric conventional treatments for cancer was. I find it cruel that there are not enough healing therapies made available to help restore the immune system. Chemotherapy and radiation are so harsh and can increase the risk of secondary cancer. If a patient chooses this option, then restoring the immune system should be the other half of her treatment. I respect the reasons people choose the therapies recommended by their doctors. Often, a prior doctor-patient relationship is already established, so trust is already there during a time when the patient is most terrified. The sense of urgency is made clear by her physician, and suddenly the patient is rushing to make a decision without getting a chance to know what other, healthier options are available.

A patient's chance of success is also going to be determined by what she does at home for self-treatment. Many patients treat themselves by researching articles on the Internet, then ordering supplements and herbs, drugs, and many other treatments without seeing a doctor first. Cost is one reason; treatment starts becoming a financial burden, the options seem fewer and fewer, and a cancer patient may see many doctors.

You have more power over your success than you may realize. Cancer treatment is a partnership, and doctors cannot make promises. Educating ourselves on the recommended treatments and alternatives is imperative. We need to do a lot of research on a drug or therapy before taking it. We must look at the pros and cons. If we are choosing an alternative approach, is it the very best? Is it aggressive enough? Ultimately, the choice is yours.

What I have learned through my fight with breast cancer is this: sometimes we are given too much to handle, and each of us copes with it differently. Adversity showed me my abilities, and it shaped me into a strong and compassionate woman. We all have the power of our perception to see a lifetime of successes and failures any way we wish. Some will see a life of many victories. Others will see many failures. Our attitude and our perception can constantly be adjusted.

In August 2018, I will have been cancer-free for seven years. I am forever grateful for alternative cancer treatments! I am living proof that we can all participate in our healing and that it is possible to choose a healthier alternative to chemotherapy. I am so grateful I did not have to endure the toxic side effects of conventional treatment.

♥ Angels for Shannon ♥

"It's amazing what a little love and teamwork can accomplish when you put your heart and mind in full flight."

- Shannon Knight

People feel good when we allow them to help us.

There were many more examples of friends who have helped me throughout my cancer journey, like Cindy, when she helped me learn about holistic healing. She provided supplements and resources for years without asking me for money. She loved with all her heart and offered the same for the rest of our circle of friends.

There was a point in my life where harsh personal circumstances forced me to leave dry and sunny California and move to Washington State, the land where hats, scarves, and raincoats were the couture fashion, where drive-through espresso places were on every corner and the misty grey days provided a reason to hang with friends by the fire playing games. All of us had spots on our cars, and it was not a desperate thing for us to park our cars in a garage when you would be getting rain the day after you washed it. Friends visited each other, and it was okay to stand by a bonfire while it was drizzling outside. Our friends were the sunshine in that misty forest. I understand how my attitude changed from hating Washington and the constant dampness that seeped to my bones to loving the closeness of friends who became family. I am grateful for the lesson and appreciate all I went through to learn the value of this kind of friends. I miss them so much and need to visit more.

It would be this same fortress of friends who would be the significant reason I am alive today. The friends who ignited everyone else to jump on board and fight with me against all odds are my angels, my daughter Jessica, my twin sister, Heather, Melody, Dawn, Cindy, Shellianne, and Mary. They are my angels and heroes who rallied for me and inspired many others to raise money to save my life. I could write a much more extensive list, but these were the women who inspired others to jump on board. They knew I did not want to do chemotherapy. I will never forget when Heather asked me again, "Shannon, if you could have whatever you wanted for cancer treatment and money was not an issue, what would you choose?" Good Lord, Heather always had a way of breaking through my barriers.

I said, "I can't just say what I want. It costs too much money."

She said, "Yes you can!"

I told her I wanted to go to CMN hospital in Mexico. She said, "Okay fine! We will raise the money and get you there one way or another." This is how "Angels for Shannon" was founded. They raised the money and got me there! My daughter Jessica, with the permission of her employer, asked coworkers to donate their coffee money to help raise money to get me to Mexico. A couple employees said they were going to donate each week until our goal was reached. This is an example of initiative from a young girl going to top management to act in a humble manner. She was grateful for every donation, and so was I.

My friend Shellianne made bracelets with crystal beads and sold them at the event. I painted wine glasses on a tray while I was spending time sick in bed.

They rallied bands together to play at Jazz Bones in Tacoma, WA. Gratitude does not even begin to cover how I feel. It is because of their call to action to love a friend and give me hope that is the reason I am alive today. They went above and beyond what I have ever experienced in any relationship in my life. I know we would do it again for any one of our friends.

They got me to CMN, and I beat stage 4 cancer without chemotherapy. I was admitted to CMN Hospital on February 7th and was completely symptom-free in August 2011. Later, October 15, 2011, my PET-CT scan confirmed that I had no evidence of disease! If not for their generosity to me their friend and sister, I would not be alive today. Angels for Shannon will always be a website resource to demonstrate to others how to hold events and go beyond crowdfunding. Every time I see the name of that website, I am reminded of who my angels are. There are some who I will never meet and get the opportunity to thank. People came to the events from all over. I want to give gratitude to all my family and friends who helped save my life including CMN Hospital and everyone who cared for a woman they did not even know. You did not just save my life; you changed it. You sparked a fire in me that wants always to pay it forward! I want to teach others how to find their heroes in their communities. We all can do it if we are transparent and humble about what we need. We can't assume we know the answers. People are continually surprising me with their giving nature. I have learned that there are a lot of good kind people out there and there is hope!

♥ *Tough Love* ♥

"Isn't it funny how day by day nothing changes, but when you look back everything is different?"

\- C.S. Lewis

The toughest love is people parting with their money and their time and giving their service when they have a loved one fighting for their life with stage 4 cancer.

When you are diagnosed with stage 4 cancer, it seems to be the end of the road. Their oncologists commonly say, "There is nothing left we can do for you." You are in shock; you go home feeling scared and tell those you love the dismal news. It's normal to break down and go through a period of momentary defeat. Sometimes, that's all it is, "a moment," perhaps a long moment, until suddenly you feel a surge of will to keep fighting. You don't want to give up! You have heard of miracle stories, where success happened even when all seemed lost! *What if I can be that miracle too! It's a long shot, but what if...*

I think rather than being hopeful, and for the purpose of protecting their own hearts from disappointment, it's easier for friends or family to say things like: "It's time for you to understand you are in denial." "Is it worth it to invest money in false hope?" "You're so desperate you can't even see or recognize a scam and how alternative doctors are just out for any money you have left!" "Is it worth all the effort of fundraising?" I had a second battle with cancer and I heard things like: "What about our friends and family? Do we burden them again this second time around?"

Some people unknowingly said things that were discouraging. I am glad I had the fortitude to keep trying and never give up. My friends granted me the freedom to be that burden, and it was so humbling. I was self-conscious and learned more of my value to them in their lives because of their compassion and generosity the entire time! They gave their hearts and souls through it all. I felt so scared of wasting their time and money but also made a "pay it forward" kind of promise to help others should I live through this! I am proof, and so are many others, that miracles are possible! Thank you for all who believed in me and my will to keep up the fight when my UCLA doctor ran out of options. The breast cancer spread to my lungs and bones, and he did all he was allowed to do. He did his best! However, it did not prove to be the best in the world for me! I never gave up.

When you walk out of that office, you are changed. After the shock wore off, and with some deep personal introspection, I realized I didn't want to give up! So I looked for another way; a healthier way. I wasn't angry that my health insurance didn't cover alternative treatment in a Mexican hospital; after all, it was not my country. So, I guess getting my affairs in order as the doctor suggested meant something completely different to me than what he had in mind. For me, it meant fundraising and getting ready for plan B: "Mexico or Bust!" Those who are still hopeful and don't feel like giving up know what I mean. It doesn't matter what they tell us. There are no guarantees in this life. So, how can anyone give up when someone has fight left to try and live?

Tough love to me is where your loved ones roll up their sleeves and say, "Really? The doctor says there is nothing else to be done?!" Then they ask you, "Do you want to keep trying? If you do, then I will fight with you. Even if it's a trip to Rome for Holy water."

Faith is the biggest part of the cancer patient's battle; they need it now more than ever! If you know someone who is sick, do all that you can to share some of your faith with him or her. The closer you are to this person, the more it will hurt if you don't.

❤ *The Love of a Twin* ❤

"I have a twin sister, who was born first and is absolutely perfect in every way—even though I am not. Oh, how grateful I am that this is probably the one thing we can agree on."

~ Shannon Knight

Me and my twin sister.

We were born on world cancer day and, ironically, both battled cancer as adults.

One September day in 2010, the UCLA doctors told me the cancer was aggressive and just spreading fast. It seemed hopeless. I had a rough morning before that appointment, and the news just heaped more fear onto what I went through that morning. I was told that unless I did the recommended chemotherapy treatments, I would just be putting my life more at risk and I had maybe months to a year left to live. I was dealing with metastatic disease spreading more to my bones, all lobes of my lungs, lymph nodes, and soft tissue. I had a staph infection in my lungs and was on IV antibiotics. I wore a fanny pack that had a 3-day supply of the antibiotics.

When I got home from my appointment with the disappointing news, my twin sister called to see how I was doing. When she asked, I said, "I'm fine!"

She said, "Really?"

I said I was going to die anyway, so what difference did it make on what I did? I was going through the anger stage of cancer grief.

She asked me if I wanted to go to the beach.

I said, "No, I can't because I have burns on my chest from where the failed radiation left my chest blistered."

She came over anyway and picked me up and drove me to the beach. She saved me that day. I was crying and so scared of dying. She was smart and played all the old 80's tunes from our high school days. She started singing to me as we went through Kanan Dune road that leads to Malibu beach. Looking back, I don't know how she did it. I would be devastated if I heard the same news about her. In Fall 2015, she battled the same type of breast cancer at stage 2. She refused the chemotherapy as well and went to the same hospital as I did in Mexico.

She's a tough girl on the outside, but I know she was breaking on the inside. On our drive to the beach, I'd start panicking and thinking about time. I was powerless over my life, and this terrified me. I cried with my head in my hands and told her, "Sis, it's not like people say about dying. They say when it's your time that you will be ready and accept it. I am terrified, sis! I am not ready to die!" I cried, and then she instructed her Tennessee lawyer friend in the back seat to give me the "purple stuff." Well, the purple stuff tasted like grape and had vodka or some other kind of alcohol in it.

I appreciate my twin sister so much for being able to take us back to our youth. I am thankful for her courage to push through when I resisted. Love is like that sometimes. We don't just give in when a loved one is pushing us out. You may have to walk through a fiery storm of emotion to get to the one you love and pull them out of the dark hole they have fallen in. You do it sometimes; that's love. Thank you, sweet sister, for your brave heart and determination.

By the time we got to the beach, I had cheered up a bit because she got me to sing songs with her (I even hung my head out the window as I sang Don Henley's "Boys of Summer"! I have gratitude for music and its ability to take you back to the happiest years of your life. I wish I could hug them and let them know how it cheered me up on that day.

We had a great day at the beach, but it felt like my final trip there; every moment was my last; every cliff, tree, and bird felt like they were getting a final goodbye. My niece Madison, my sister's daughter, was happy to be playing by the sea with her colorful shovel and bucket. She was so innocent and unaware of what I was going through, and I looked at her knowing she had such a hopeful future. Madison was beautiful and wise beyond her years and would say things to cheer me up. She senses things no matter what, which I find amazing to this day. Thank you, Madison, for your precious way of bringing me back to the present every time I let my fear get the best of me by overthinking about the future.

Had I known then about alternative cancer treatment, I would have walked out of that doctor's appointment knowing they were wrong and that there was a healthier alternative than their limited resources of conventional treatments. Fear would have been replaced with excitement, and we would have built the grandest sand castle that day.

♥ A Plea to God ♥

"She became a giant on her knees. With a sword in one hand she battled the enemies of death and disease, and with the other hand stretched toward heaven she kept beseeching God's help and His mercy."

\- Bishop T. D. Jakes

Later that day on the beach, as the sun began to lower, I took a walk. I guess the alcohol had worn off, and I felt I was going to lose it emotionally. I just needed to come to terms with death, and this required a private conversation with God. I walked under the dock to the other side of paradise cove in Malibu, I laid down on the sand, and I stared up at the sky; it felt more like a part of me than any other moment in my life. It almost felt like it was falling closer to me and I was becoming part of the sky. I had never experienced that feeling before. There I lay alone—just me and God and all the angels in the sand. I had no towel or blanket, just the clothes I wore, a long, green maxi skirt and a long sleeved, white shirt to protect my radiation-burned skin from the sun. My mind was flooded with memories of all my loved ones who had already passed before. Some died from cancer. I was frightened but felt a little bit of comfort knowing they would greet me on the other side when it was time. They'd be waiting for me in heaven.

I was terrified laying there. Acceptance of death crept in a little bit, but it was odd; it felt all wrong. I felt like I had so much still that I had to do. I felt a sudden passion run through me with the Lord and I had a conversation with Him that day. I made a promise to God, and it was a big one. I prayed so hard and pleaded with Him with determination.

Here is the most real and vulnerable moment of my life. It doesn't get more real than this. I did what I am sure many of us with faith do; I pleaded because I was sad to leave my kids, and I felt like I still had unfinished things to do. I felt a purpose to stay, and it was stronger than ever. I begged God as tears poured down my cheeks. "Please let me stay; I swear to you I will make my life worth more than 10 volunteers. Just let me show you that I can make my life purposeful. I can help people! Let me stay and beat this cancer my way, the healthy way. Let me help other cancer patients. I can do so much more here than I can in heaven. Let me show you!" I don't know where that falls in line with being a good Christian, and I just felt I needed to have this serious talk with God. I've always believed in God's will, but anyone that knows me knows I'll have my say in a situation that I feel strongly about.

The gratitude I feel for being alive eight years after that conversation is the most gratitude I have ever had. I feel it every day. Faith is vital in everything I do. I am keeping the promise I made. It wasn't really a deal; it was a calling, and I want my life to be a life that serves others. What happened that day has caused my life to change forever. I thank you, Lord, for all the blessings in my life for getting me through the darkest days and giving me a chance to show you that I can do so much more than I ever thought I was able to do until I got sick. You revealed all my abilities and have been equipping me ever since so I can keep my promise to help others in their battles with cancer.

♥ *Louie* ♥

"If the entire world showed their appreciation as much as my dog Louie does for everything, we would have the answer to world peace: humility and gratitude."

- Shannon Knight

I have a little Italian Greyhound dog named Louie. He has been in my life through most of my journey battling cancer twice. I think about all the comfort he has brought to me when I was alone. I can go deep into the subject of how a pet can relieve stress for the sick. There is science everywhere to back this up. To sum up the greatest thing about Louie and why I am so grateful for the 11 years of his companionship is this: Louie knows how to love unconditionally. I can be in bed, sick, scared, and depressed, wearing the same PJs for two days in a row, and he will still be the comforter. You get a friend in your room looking at you in such a state, and they will try to fix you—or never come back if you smell bad enough! Louie will not criticize you and still offer the same comfort, and because of the consistency in their affection and loyalty, I know there is a great place for pets in heaven!

I heard a joke once: If you were to lock your dog and your spouse in the trunk of your car and return an hour later, who would be happy to see you? Your dog would! We can learn a lot from our pets—although I prefer never learning how to accept being locked in a trunk for an hour! Though I do find myself trying harder because of my dog. I have had to take him to the vet many times for serious health issues. On February 14, Valentine's Day, Louie had a serious surgery to remove cancerous tumors from his 17-pound little body. There were complications with the surgery, and I almost lost my little buddy. I have learned to look past what it costs to get him well again. I am so grateful for the vet, surgeon, and everyone ever involved in Louie's recovery. He is loved by many and loves them right back.

❤ *The Science of Gratitude* ❤

"So you think this is just another day in your life? It's not just another day. It's the one day that was given to you...today."

~ Br. David Steindl-Rast

Gratitude is formally defined as "the quality of being thankful; readiness to show appreciation for and to return kindness."[1] Gratitude is not just a random expression of thanks, but rather a mindful activity that has been proven to have measurable effects on your mental, emotional, and physical health. Practicing gratitude on a daily basis is important and has the potential to change your life!

What Studies Have Shown: The Power of Gratitude

Gratitude has been studied through a scientific lens many times, especially over the past decade, and the results, which have been largely replicated, show that expressing gratitude has positive physical, mental, and emotional results. For example, a study conducted by the University of California, Berkeley has revealed many of the positive benefits that people experience if they express gratitude: [2]

Physical

- Have stronger immune systems
- Are less bothered by aches and pains
- Have lower blood pressure
- Exercise more and take better care of their health
- Sleep longer and feel more refreshed upon waking

Psychological

- Attain higher levels of positive emotions
- Feel more alert, alive, and awake
- Experience more joy and pleasure
- Have more optimism and happiness

Social

- Tend to be more helpful, generous, and compassionate
- Forgive more often
- Are more outgoing
- Feel less lonely and isolated

A separate, independent study carried out by Robert A. Emmons, Ph.D., at the University of California at Davis and his colleague Mike McCullough at the University of Miami further supports this. Their experiment: [3]

"...randomly assigned participants were given one of three tasks. Each week, participants kept a short journal. The gratitude group briefly described five things they were grateful for that had occurred in the past week, the hassle group recorded five daily hassles from the previous week that displeased them, and the neutral group was asked to list five events or circumstances that affected them, but they were not told whether to focus on the positive or on the negative. Ten weeks later, participants in the gratitude group felt better about their lives as a whole and were a full 25 percent happier than the hassled group. They reported fewer health complaints and exercised an average of 1.5 hours more."

Thus, it can be concluded that gratitude helps people to feel happier and more energized in their daily lives. Gratitude is also linked into higher quality of mental and emotional health.

Notably, expressing gratitude can greatly affect the quality of life for cancer warriors by helping them to overcome trauma. "A 2006 study published in *Behavior Research and Therapy* found that Vietnam War Veterans with higher levels of gratitude experienced lower rates of Post-Traumatic Stress Disorder. A 2003 study published in the *Journal of Personality and Social Psychology* found that gratitude was a major contributor to resilience following the terrorist attacks on September 11. Recognizing all you have to be thankful for – even during the worst times of your life – fosters resilience."[4] Such resilience helps cancer warriors to fight harder, stronger, and longer.

Implementing Gratitude

Published "research by UC Davis psychologist Robert Emmons, author of *Thanks!: How the new Science of Gratitude Can Make You Happier*, shows that simply keeping a gratitude journal—regularly writing brief reflections on moments for which we're thankful—can significantly increase well-being and life satisfaction."[5] This task can have amazing, long-lasting, and far-reaching results and requires very little; you can complete this with a pen and notebook, on your phone or laptop, or even on a scrap piece of paper. The important aspect is that you take the time to mindfully reflect on what you are truly thankful for. Your list may start out simply, with gratitude for a roof over your head and the ability to write things down. Over time, you will reach further; your list may become more elaborate or extend beyond a page. There are no rules aside from listing things that you are *truly and sincerely grateful for.*

Another way in which you can implement gratitude expression into your daily life is through letters, or quick texts. Maybe you will make a promise to yourself that you will send out a quick text message (or email) when you first wake up to someone that you are grateful for; maybe you will elaborate further and choose to write a letter that reflects on your gratitude at the end of your day, before you go to bed. This is ultimately up to you: you know yourself better than anyone else, so you have the right to dictate how, when, where, and why you would like to express your gratitude.

❤ Using Your Gratitude Journal ❤

Gratitude can have such a positive impact on our lives.

It quite possibly could be that *gratitude* is one of the most overlooked methods to obtaining an abundant life. When we are grateful for everyday blessings, we set ourselves on a path that opens doors to everyday miracles.

A *gratitude journal* is a great first step to bringing more abundance to your life. The effort and thoughtfulness you put into this journal, you will definitely see returned to you. If you are going through difficult challenges in your life, it may be hard for you to find five things a day to be grateful for, but I assure you that if you give this book a chance, you will begin to notice the wonderful people and things around you that you might be taking for granted.

Reflect on my personal anecdote of how I used 5 minutes of my day to turn my entire mental attitude around. I was honest in my story—I explained how angry and frustrated I truly was, yet through gratitude, I was able to slowly transition to a state of appreciation, furthermore becoming happier through this exercise. This is a modest task, but when you make it part of your daily routine, you will notice large aspects of your life changing in amazing ways.

It only takes 5 minutes to write a list of 5 things that you are thankful for in a day, but the benefits will far outlast the time that you initially put into it. You can start with this 40-day gratitude journal. Begin today! Take 5 minutes to mentally recognize things, people, or memories that you are thankful for and write down 5 of them in your journal.

Example:

> Today, 1/7/17, I am grateful for:
> 1. Today is a sunny day
> 2. Nurturing staff
> 3. Modern technology that allows me to communicate and keep in touch with loved ones
> 4. A soft blanket
> 5. My gratitude journal to keep me mindful of all of life's blessings

Use the template pages that follow to begin your own gratitude journal. I have provided space for 40 entries total, and I have included a quote for a little extra motivation! I have also included 40 exercises to supplement the journal and prompt expression of gratitude in your day-to-day life. Don't feel bad if it is hard to think of five things some days—it happens to all of us sometimes, but this book will help you push past it. Eventually, you will be able to elaborate on the things you are grateful for. See this journal as the starting place where abundance begins to flow into your life—right here, in these pages.

"It is not happy people who are grateful; it is grateful people who are happy."

Let the journey begin!

Wishing you an abundant life and everyday blessings,

Shannon

Your

Gratitude Journal

♥ Day 1 ♥

"Gratitude is being able to see the blessings, even if you are looking at them through tears."

- Shannon Knight

Today, _____, I am grateful for:

1. _____

   _____

   _____

2. _____

   _____

   _____

3. _____

   _____

   _____

4. _____

   _____

   _____

5. _____

   _____

   _____

For a moment, I want you to close your eyes and just relax. Think of something a family member or friend did for you without being asked. How did it make you feel? Draw a picture that shows your feelings or write down several words that express how it made you feel.

♥ Day 2 ♥

"Gratitude turns what we have into enough, and more. It turns denial into acceptance, chaos into order, confusion into clarity...it makes sense of our past, brings peace for today, and creates a better vision for tomorrow."

- Melody Beatty

Today, _____, I am grateful for:

1. _____
   _____
   _____

2. _____
   _____
   _____

3. _____
   _____
   _____

4. _____
   _____
   _____

5. _____
   _____
   _____

If home is where the heart is, how much heart do we put in our homes? Look around your home and find things that you are grateful for. You can do something artistic and take photos of small things like a toothbrush or the entire house or backyard. Make a collage or photo book with these photos. Write about the things that you found that inspire you.

_____

_____

_____

_____

_____

_____

_____

_____

_____

_____

_____

_____

_____

_____

_____

_____

_____

♥ Day 3 ♥

"So much has been given to me. I have no time to ponder over that which has been denied."

- Helen Keller

Today, _____, I am grateful for:

1. _____

_____

_____

2. _____

_____

_____

3. _____

_____

_____

4. _____

_____

_____

5. _____

_____

_____

When is the last time you sent out a letter of thanks? Think of someone that did something for you and thank them in an email, a phone call, or a thank you card or gift. Use the space provided to draft what you are going to say or write to them.

_____

_____

_____

_____

_____

_____

_____

_____

_____

_____

_____

_____

_____

_____

_____

_____

_____

_____

♥ Day 4 ♥

"Let gratitude be the pillow upon which you kneel to say your nightly prayer. And let faith be the bridge you build to overcome evil and welcome good."

~ Maya Angelou

Today, _____, I am grateful for:

1. _____
_____
_____

2. _____
_____
_____

3. _____
_____
_____

4. _____
_____
_____

5. _____
_____
_____

Random act of gratitude. Challenge yourself and send a thank you to a favorite place you do business with. What is unique about this business? How do they make you feel as a customer?

_____

_____

_____

_____

_____

_____

_____

_____

_____

_____

_____

_____

_____

_____

_____

_____

_____

_____

_____

_____

♥ Day 5 ♥

"It is impossible to be grateful and depressed in the same moment."
~ Naomi Williams

Today, _____, I am grateful for:

1. _____
_____
_____

2. _____
_____
_____

3. _____
_____
_____

4. _____
_____
_____

5. _____
_____
_____

Make a gratitude jar. Get a little note pad and a big jar you can decorate with words of love and gratitude. Every time you feel extra gratitude for a blessing in your life. Write it down and put it in your jar. You can involve your entire family and read them out loud at the end of each week. Use the space provided to draw a picture of your gratitude jar. Art can inspire us!

♥ Day 6 ♥

"Piglet noticed that even though he had a Very Small Heart, it could hold a rather large amount of gratitude."

\- A. A. Milne

Today, _____, I am grateful for:

1. _____

_____

_____

2. _____

_____

_____

3. _____

_____

_____

4. _____

_____

_____

5. _____

_____

_____

Plan a day to take a nature walk somewhere. Take pictures of the nature all around you. Say thank you to the tree for providing shade or its colorful autumn leaves. Say, thank you to the changing sky in all its color and splendor. Say thank you to anything that you may be taking for granted. Write down what you are thankful for in your journal.

_____
_____
_____
_____
_____
_____
_____
_____
_____
_____
_____
_____
_____
_____
_____
_____
_____
_____

♥ Day 7 ♥

"True forgiveness is when you can say, 'Thank you for that experience.'"

\- Oprah Winfrey

Today, _____, I am grateful for:

1. _____

_____

_____

2. _____

_____

_____

3. _____

_____

_____

4. _____

_____

_____

5. _____

_____

_____

Say thank you without getting caught! That's right! Put a note on a friend's door or co-worker's desk. Let them know how grateful you are for things you appreciate and do not sign it. Use the space provided to list important people who you would like to thank anonymously.

_____

_____

_____

_____

_____

_____

_____

_____

_____

_____

_____

_____

_____

_____

_____

_____

_____

_____

♥ Day 8 ♥

"Thank you is the best prayer one can say. I say that one a lot. Thank you expresses extreme gratitude, humility, understanding."

~ Alice Walker

Today, _____, I am grateful for:

1. _____

_____

_____

2. _____

_____

_____

3. _____

_____

_____

4. _____

_____

_____

5. _____

_____

_____

If you have social media like Facebook, make a gratitude photo album. Whenever you feel gratitude about something, take a picture or find a picture that expresses what you are grateful for and post in your gratitude album. Make a list here about things that you could photograph that would inspire feelings of appreciation.

_____

_____

_____

_____

_____

_____

_____

_____

_____

_____

_____

_____

_____

_____

_____

_____

_____

_____

♥ Day 9 ♥

"Look at everything as though you were seeing it for the first or last time, then your time on earth will be filled with glory."

- Betty Smith

Today, _____ , I am grateful for:

1. _____
_____
_____

2. _____
_____
_____

3. _____
_____
_____

4. _____
_____
_____

5. _____
_____
_____

Write a gratitude poem or Haiku. A Haiku is fun, the first and last lines of a Haiku have 5 syllables and the middle line has 7 syllables. The lines rarely rhyme.

_____

_____

_____

_____

_____

_____

_____

_____

_____

_____

_____

_____

_____

_____

_____

_____

_____

_____

♥ Day 10 ♥

"Appreciation can change a day, even change a life. You willingness to put it into words is all that is necessary."

~ Margaret Cousins

Today, _____, I am grateful for:

1. _____

_____

_____

2. _____

_____

_____

3. _____

_____

_____

4. _____

_____

_____

5. _____

_____

_____

Write down your favorite song that has to do with gratitude. What is it about this song, or music in general, that inspires you? What would life be like without music?

_____
_____
_____
_____
_____
_____
_____
_____
_____
_____
_____
_____
_____
_____
_____
_____
_____
_____

♥ Day 11 ♥

"Spread love everywhere you go. Let no one ever come to you without leaving happier."

- Mother Teresa

Today, _____, I am grateful for:

1. _____

_____

_____

2. _____

_____

_____

3. _____

_____

_____

4. _____

_____

_____

5. _____

_____

_____

Write your own daily thanks prayer here. You are the author of it and can put as much time and creativity as you wish into it.

_____

_____

_____

_____

_____

_____

_____

_____

_____

_____

_____

_____

_____

_____

_____

_____

_____

_____

_____

_____

_____

❤ Day 12 ❤

"Gratitude and attitude are not challenges. They are choices."
~ Robert Braathe

Today, _____, I am grateful for:

1. _____

_____

_____

2. _____

_____

_____

3. _____

_____

_____

4. _____

_____

_____

5. _____

_____

_____

If you have children, even adult children, write them a thank you card. Mail it to them if they live outside of your home, or leave it on their bed if they are still young. How do your children, or children in general, inspire feelings of thankfulness?

_____

_____

_____

_____

_____

_____

_____

_____

_____

_____

_____

_____

_____

_____

_____

_____

_____

_____

_____

♥ Day 13 ♥

"You won't be happy with more until you're happy with what you've got."

- Viki King

Today, _____, I am grateful for:

1. _____

_____

_____

2. _____

_____

_____

3. _____

_____

_____

4. _____

_____

_____

5. _____

_____

_____

This week, buy a balloon, candy, or flowers for someone you are especially grateful for and give it to them. If they live out of town, have something delivered with a card of gratitude. What is it about this person that you are grateful for? How is your life better because of this person?

_____

_____

_____

_____

_____

_____

_____

_____

_____

_____

_____

_____

_____

_____

_____

_____

_____

_____

_____

_____

♥ Day 14 ♥

"Gratitude changes the pangs of memory into a tranquil joy."
- Dietrich Bonhoeffer

Today, _____, I am grateful for:

1. _____
_____
_____

2. _____
_____
_____

3. _____
_____
_____

4. _____
_____
_____

5. _____
_____
_____

Put a picture of you when you were a child up on your mirror or somewhere else you frequent. Talk to her and tell her all the things you appreciate about her. Tell her how grateful you are for all the things she has done. List them here, and try not to leave anything out!

_____

_____

_____

_____

_____

_____

_____

_____

_____

_____

_____

_____

_____

_____

_____

_____

_____

_____

_____

♥ Day 15 ♥

"To speak gratitude is courteous and pleasant, to enact gratitude is generous and noble, but to live gratitude is to touch Heaven."

-Johannes A. Gaertner

Today, _____, I am grateful for:

1. _____

_____

_____

2. _____

_____

_____

3. _____

_____

_____

4. _____

_____

_____

5. _____

_____

_____

What is the most positive change you made in your life over the last year that you are thankful for?

_____

_____

_____

_____

_____

_____

_____

_____

_____

_____

_____

_____

_____

_____

_____

_____

_____

_____

_____

_____

♥ Day 16 ♥

"When we take resentment and anger and replace it with gratitude, we feel an abundance of light and love filling those dark places of our hearts."

~ Shannon Knight

Today, _____, I am grateful for:

1. _____
_____
_____

2. _____
_____
_____

3. _____
_____
_____

4. _____
_____
_____

5. _____
_____
_____

What is one small thing you use every day that you are grateful for? How would your life be different without this one item? List other small things that you take for granted.

_____
_____
_____
_____
_____
_____
_____
_____
_____
_____
_____
_____
_____
_____
_____
_____
_____
_____

♥ Day 17 ♥

"Whatever we are waiting for—peace of mind, contentment, grace, the inner awareness of simple abundance—it will surely come to us, but only when we are ready to receive it with an open and grateful heart."

~ Sarah Ban Breathnach

Today, _____, I am grateful for:

1. _____

   _____

   _____

2. _____

   _____

   _____

3. _____

   _____

   _____

4. _____

   _____

   _____

5. _____

   _____

   _____

Think about what in nature you are grateful for and why. (The ocean, mountains, snow, or sunshine. Maybe it's a starry sky or the sunset.)

_____

_____

_____

_____

_____

_____

_____

_____

_____

_____

_____

_____

_____

_____

_____

_____

_____

_____

_____

♥ Day 18 ♥

"What a wonderful life I have had! I only wish I'd realized it sooner."
- Collette

Today, _____ , I am grateful for:

1. _____

_____

_____

2. _____

_____

_____

3. _____

_____

_____

4. _____

_____

_____

5. _____

_____

_____

Take a moment, close your eyes, and imagine life without music. What music would you miss the most and are thankful to be able to listen to. Why?

_____

_____

_____

_____

_____

_____

_____

_____

_____

_____

_____

_____

_____

_____

_____

_____

_____

_____

_____

_____

_____

♥ Day 19 ♥

"Dwell on the beauty of life. Watch the stars, and see yourself running with them."

- Marcus Aurelius

Today, _____ , I am grateful for:

1. _____

_____

_____

2. _____

_____

_____

3. _____

_____

_____

4. _____

_____

_____

5. _____

_____

_____

Who has done something recently that turned your frown upside down and made you smile? What was it? Send them a thank you.

_____

_____

_____

_____

_____

_____

_____

_____

_____

_____

_____

_____

_____

_____

_____

_____

_____

_____

_____

_____

♥ Day 20 ♥

"Train yourself never to put off the word or action for the expression of gratitude."
- Albert Schweitzer

Today, _____, I am grateful for:

1. _____

_____

_____

2. _____

_____

_____

3. _____

_____

_____

4. _____

_____

_____

5. _____

_____

_____

When was the last time you laughed a lot. What was it that made you laugh?

_____

_____

_____

_____

_____

_____

_____

_____

_____

_____

_____

_____

_____

_____

_____

_____

_____

_____

_____

❤ Day 21 ❤

"The hardest arithmetic to master is that which enables us to count our blessings."

~ Eric Hoffer

Today, _____ , I am grateful for:

1. _____

_____

_____

2. _____

_____

_____

3. _____

_____

_____

4. _____

_____

_____

5. _____

_____

_____

Today's challenge! List someone in your life who is difficult to get along with. Recognize at least two qualities in that person you are grateful for.

_____

_____

_____

_____

_____

_____

_____

_____

_____

_____

_____

_____

_____

_____

_____

_____

_____

_____

_____

_____

_____

♥ Day 22 ♥

"Gratitude doesn't change the scenery. It merely washes clean the glass you look through so you can clearly see the colors."
~ Richelle E. Goodrich

Today, _____, I am grateful for:

1. _____

_____

_____

2. _____

_____

_____

3. _____

_____

_____

4. _____

_____

_____

5. _____

_____

_____

Where is your favorite spot to sit at home and read or maybe write in this journal? Is it your sofa? Outside on a porch swing? Or maybe it's at the table with a friend or spouse having breakfast.

_____

_____

_____

_____

_____

_____

_____

_____

_____

_____

_____

_____

_____

_____

_____

_____

_____

♥ Day 23 ♥

"If you concentrate on finding whatever is good in every situation, you will discover that your life will suddenly be filled with gratitude, a feeling that nurtures the soul."

~ Harold Kushner

Today, _____ , I am grateful for:

1. _____

_____

_____

2. _____

_____

_____

3. _____

_____

_____

4. _____

_____

_____

5. _____

_____

_____

What dessert are you grateful for, and when is the last time you enjoyed it? Write down your favorite dessert recipe.

_____

_____

_____

_____

_____

_____

_____

_____

_____

_____

_____

_____

_____

_____

_____

_____

_____

_____

_____

_____

♥ Day 24 ♥

"If you want to turn your life around, try thankfulness. It will change your life mightily."

~ Gerald Good

Today, _____, I am grateful for:

1. _____

_____

_____

2. _____

_____

_____

3. _____

_____

_____

4. _____

_____

_____

5. _____

_____

_____

Write about one teacher or professor you are grateful for. How did he or she inspire you?

_____

_____

_____

_____

_____

_____

_____

_____

_____

_____

_____

_____

_____

_____

_____

_____

_____

_____

_____

_____

_____

_____

♥ Day 25 ♥

"Gratitude is a currency that we can mint for ourselves and spend without fear of bankruptcy."

- Fred de Witt Van Amburgh

Today, _____, I am grateful for:

1. _____
_____
_____

2. _____
_____
_____

3. _____
_____
_____

4. _____
_____
_____

5. _____
_____
_____

What do you appreciate about the weather today?

♥ Day 26 ♥

"Gratitude is riches. Complaint is poverty."
- Doris Day

Today, _____ , I am grateful for:

1. _____

_____

_____

2. _____

_____

_____

3. _____

_____

_____

4. _____

_____

_____

5. _____

_____

_____

What is one talent or skill you have that you are thankful for? (You are a good listener, you are a good gardener, a great photographer or artist.)

_____

_____

_____

_____

_____

_____

_____

_____

_____

_____

_____

_____

_____

_____

_____

_____

_____

_____

_____

♥ Day 27 ♥

"Do not indulge in dreams of having what you have not, but reckon up the chief of blessings you do possess, and then thankfully remember how you would crave for them if they were not yours."

- Marcus Aurelius

Today, _____, I am grateful for:

1. _____

_____

_____

2. _____

_____

_____

3. _____

_____

_____

4. _____

_____

_____

5. _____

_____

_____

What adversity have you experienced in your past that you can be thankful for? (I know this is tough, but it is through past adversity that we discover new abilities within ourselves.)

_____

_____

_____

_____

_____

_____

_____

_____

_____

_____

_____

_____

_____

_____

_____

_____

_____

_____

♥ Day 28 ♥

"When we have lost that fire in us and see nothing more than a glowing ember, we must be grateful for our last breath of hope. Gratitude in the things we take for granted can be the very things that rekindle our life."

- Shannon Knight

Today, _____, I am grateful for:

1. _____
_____
_____

2. _____
_____
_____

3. _____
_____
_____

4. _____
_____
_____

5. _____
_____
_____

What is your favorite clothing item that you are grateful for? (Favorite comfy sweater, favorite pajamas, or how about a cozy robe in the morning?)

_____

_____

_____

_____

_____

_____

_____

_____

_____

_____

_____

_____

_____

_____

_____

_____

_____

_____

_____

_____

♥ Day 29 ♥

"We would worry less if we praised more. Thanksgiving is the enemy of discontent and dissatisfaction."

~ H.A. Ironside

Today, _____, I am grateful for:

1. _____

_____

_____

2. _____

_____

_____

3. _____

_____

_____

4. _____

_____

_____

5. _____

_____

_____

What one thing have you been taking for granted each day that you can be thankful for? (Your computer, your smartphone, your coffee machine, your friendly neighbor who always says good morning...and that's before you even leave the house!)

_____

_____

_____

_____

_____

_____

_____

_____

_____

_____

_____

_____

_____

_____

_____

_____

_____

♥ *Day 30* ♥

"No one who achieves success does so without acknowledging the help of others. The wise and confident acknowledge this help with gratitude."

- Alfred North Whitehead

Today, _____, I am grateful for:

1. _____

_____

_____

2. _____

_____

_____

3. _____

_____

_____

4. _____

_____

_____

5. _____

_____

_____

What activities or hobbies would you miss if you were unable to do them?

_____
_____
_____
_____
_____
_____
_____
_____
_____
_____
_____
_____
_____
_____
_____
_____
_____
_____
_____
_____
_____
_____

♥ Day 31 ♥

"No one can steal contentment, joy, gratitude or peace—we have to give it away."

~ Kristin Armstrong

Today, _____, I am grateful for:

1. _____

_____

_____

2. _____

_____

_____

3. _____

_____

_____

4. _____

_____

_____

5. _____

_____

_____

List parts of your body that you're grateful for and why.
(Arms because you have the ability to hug, legs because
you have the ability to dance or walk.)

_____

_____

_____

_____

_____

_____

_____

_____

_____

_____

_____

_____

_____

_____

_____

_____

_____

_____

♥ Day 32 ♥

"Feeling gratitude and not expressing it is like wrapping a present and not giving it."

- William Arthur Ward

Today, _____, I am grateful for:

1. _____

_____

_____

2. _____

_____

_____

3. _____

_____

_____

4. _____

_____

_____

5. _____

_____

_____

What is your favorite meal that you are most thankful for? (Tacos? Lasagna? A holiday meal?) Write down the recipe and think of someone that you would like to cook this meal for to express thanks.

_____

_____

_____

_____

_____

_____

_____

_____

_____

_____

_____

_____

_____

_____

_____

_____

_____

_____

♥ Day 33 ♥

"As we express our gratitude, we must never forget that the highest appreciation is not to utter words, but to live by them."

~ John F. Kennedy

Today, _____, I am grateful for:

1. _____

_____

_____

2. _____

_____

_____

3. _____

_____

_____

4. _____

_____

_____

5. _____

_____

_____

What is your favorite thing you are grateful for each morning in your routine? (A hot cup of coffee or tea, cuddling with someone—or even a pet) Write about its significance to you.

_____

_____

_____

_____

_____

_____

_____

_____

_____

_____

_____

_____

_____

_____

_____

_____

_____

_____

_____

♥ Day 34 ♥

"Gratitude is not only the greatest of virtues, but the parent of all others."

~ Cicero

Today, _____, I am grateful for:

1. _____
   _____
   _____

2. _____
   _____
   _____

3. _____
   _____
   _____

4. _____
   _____
   _____

5. _____
   _____
   _____

What have you learned this last month that you are grateful for?

_____

_____

_____

_____

_____

_____

_____

_____

_____

_____

_____

_____

_____

_____

_____

_____

_____

_____

_____

_____

♥ Day 35 ♥

"The soul that gives thanks can find comfort in everything; the soul that complains can find comfort in nothing."

\- Hannah Whitall Smith

Today, _____, I am grateful for:

1. _____

_____

_____

2. _____

_____

_____

3. _____

_____

_____

4. _____

_____

_____

5. _____

_____

_____

Answer the following at the end of your day:

What one thing do I have to be grateful for that others wish they had?

_____

_____

_____

Who inspired me today?

_____

_____

_____

Who did I inspire?

_____

_____

_____

What made me laugh today?

_____

_____

_____

What's the best thing that happened today?

_____

_____

_____

♥ Day 36 ♥

"Gratitude is a debt which ought to be paid, but which none have a right to expect."

- Jean-Jaques Rousseau

Today, _____, I am grateful for:

1. _____
_____
_____

2. _____
_____
_____

3. _____
_____
_____

4. _____
_____
_____

5. _____
_____
_____

Turn an ungrateful thought into a grateful one.

<u>Example:</u>

Ungrateful thought: *Today my sister called me too many times. She kept interrupting me while I worked and broke my concentration.*

Grateful thought: *I am so grateful I have my sister! She is a blessing and she makes me laugh when I am feeling sad.*

Ungrateful thought: _____

_____

_____

_____

_____

_____

_____

_____

_____

Grateful thought: _____

_____

_____

_____

_____

_____

_____

♥ Day 37 ♥

"The only people with whom you should try to get even are those who have helped you."

\- John E Southard

Today, _____, I am grateful for:

1. _____

_____

_____

2. _____

_____

_____

3. _____

_____

_____

4. _____

_____

_____

5. _____

_____

_____

Gratitude treasure chest: Create a box, a drawer or a chest designated for thank you presents. In this drawer you will wrap little things you purchase to show appreciation for you on a day when you are feeling down. Self-compassion is important. Wrap up a piece of candy, a book of inspirational quotes, bubble bath, or popcorn for a movie. You can even write a letter of gratitude to yourself to remind yourself of your own qualities. Be creative. These gifts will be your treasure on a tough day. Draw a picture of your treasure chest here.

♥ Day 38 ♥

"Things turn out best for people who make the best of the way things turn out."
- John Wooden

Today, _____, I am grateful for:

1. _____

_____

_____

2. _____

_____

_____

3. _____

_____

_____

4. _____

_____

_____

5. _____

_____

_____

Buy a piece of art for your home to hang on the wall to remind yourself to be grateful. You can find the most amazing art to fit any home decor with the words "Be Grateful" on it. Sketch a room in your house with your newest art installation.

♥ Day 39 ♥

"No duty is more urgent than that of returning thanks."
- James Allen

Today, _____, I am grateful for:

1. _____
   _____
   _____

2. _____
   _____
   _____

3. _____
   _____
   _____

4. _____
   _____
   _____

5. _____
   _____
   _____

Send an anonymous thank you card to your employer, kid's teacher, or even the church clergy. Thank them for what they contribute in your life, in your family's life and let them know how grateful you are. Be sure to write a few details. Draft your thank you card in the space provided.

_____

_____

_____

_____

_____

_____

_____

_____

_____

_____

_____

_____

_____

_____

_____

_____

♥ Day 40 ♥

"The more thankful you are each day, the more miracles you will witness."

\- Shannon Knight

Today, _____, I am grateful for:

1. _____
   _____
   _____

2. _____
   _____
   _____

3. _____
   _____
   _____

4. _____
   _____
   _____

5. _____
   _____
   _____

Begin a story of gratitude with a voice recorder. There are voice activated recorders you can purchase for under $40. You can record special times where you felt grateful and you can talk about how gratitude is changing your life. One day your story will help another person. You can even write a book! Write some ideas for your story in the space provided.

_____

_____

_____

_____

_____

_____

_____

_____

_____

_____

_____

_____

_____

_____

_____

_____

_____

_____

Now that you have completed your fortieth day of reflection, look back and see how quickly you have created more abundance in your life by having an attitude of gratitude. Here's to the next forty days of thankfulness and more... and keep your eyes out for my next gratitude journal. ☺

For more information and life-empowerment resources, please visit:

www.shannonknight.com

Wishing you an abundant life,

Shannon

♥ About the Author ♥

Shannon Knight survived breast cancer not once but twice, including a harrowing battle with a recurrence of stage 4 in 2010. Shannon defeated cancer without ever using chemotherapy; instead she traveled to CMN Hospital in Mexico to explore healthy alternatives, which saved her life.

Giving hope to those who have lost it, propping up those for one last go at battling cancer when they need it, and rooting for those whom everyone else has given up on is Shannon's mission.

As a Christian, Shannon takes refuge in her faith. The calling came when she thought she wasn't ready, but she knew God would be there during her darkest days. During her battle with cancer, Shannon prayed and pleaded for a chance to stay and help others. God gave her the gift of living once more. Shannon emerged from the darkness into a new life, one in which she would serve others even more than before—a life dedicated to giving back and helping to shine the light of love, faith, and understanding to those who are in the fight of their lives. Shannon's message is clear: be grateful for those closest to your heart.

❤ References ❤

1. shannonknight.com

2. CMN Hospital (Alternative Cancer treatment) http://www.cmnact.com/

3. "Gratitude," *Merriam-Webster.*

4. Emmons, Robert. "Why Gratitude is Good." *Greater Good, UC Berkeley.* 2010.

3. Robbins, Ocean. "The Neuroscience of Why Gratitude Makes Us Healthier." *The Huffington Post.* 2011.

4. Morin, Amy. "7 Scientifically Proven Benefits of Gratitude That Motivate You to Give Thanks Year-Round." *Forbes.* 2014.

5. Carpenter, Derrick MAPP. "The Science Behind Gratitude (and How It Can Change Your Life). *Happify Daily.*